DRIVE

THE FIRST QUARTET

Other Works by
Lorna Dee Cervantes:

Emplumada
(American Book Award)

*From the Cables of Genocide:
Poems on Love and Hunger*
(Paterson Prize,
Latino Literature Award)

*Y la tierra no los olvidó /
And the Earth Did Not Forget Them*

DRIVE

THE FIRST QUARTET

Lorna Dee Cervantes

San Antonio, Texas
2006

First Edition
ISBN: 0-930324-54-4 (hardback)
Converted ISBN: 978-0-930324-54-4

Wings Press
627 E. Guenther • San Antonio, Texas 78210
Phone/fax: (210) 271-7805 • www.wingspress.com

Library of Congress Cataloging-in-Publication Data

Cervantes, Lorna Dee.
  Drive : the first quartet / Lorna Dee Cervantes.-- 1st ed.
    p. cm.
  ISBN-13: 978-0-930324-54-4 (hardback : alk. paper)
  ISBN-10: 0-930324-54-4 (hardback : alk. paper)
  1. Indigenous peoples--Poetry. I. Title.
  PS3553.E79D75 2006
  813'.54--dc22
                                    2006018878

No public funding was used in the production of this book.

Contents

Acknowledgments:

Many of these poems have appeared in earlier forms, and have been distributed widely over the internet. Some titles have been changed, but are cited below by the title used in specific publications.

"Bananas" was first published in *Daughters of the Fifth Sun*, 1995, and has since appeared in numerous other anthologies, including *Chicana Criticism, Chicana Creativity*, 1996, and *The Heath Anthology of American Literature*, 1998, and most recently in *Word of Mouth: Poems Featured on NPR's All Things Considered*, 2003. "Bananas" and "Coffee" appeared in the chapbook, *Y la tierra no los olvidó / And the Earth Did Not Forget Them* (Wings, 2005). An earlier version of "Coffee" was included in the newsletter, *Dark Night: field notes* (1998). "Tasco" appeared in *Women in the Arts* (Fall 2005).

The following poems appeared as cited: "For My Ancestors Adobed In the Walls of the Santa Barbara Mission" in *Divide*, 2004; "To We Who Were Saved by the Stars" in *Prentice Hall Anthology of Latino Literature, 2001;* "Imagine" (winner, "Galway Kinnell's Word Hoard Challenge," "Poems After the Attack," and "Palestine" ("We Have A Country of Words")) in Poetry.About.Com, 2001 ; "Summer Ends Too Soon" and "Poet's Progress" in Bill Moyers' *Fooling With Words: A Celebration of Poets and Their Craft*, 1999; "Isla Mujeres," "A un Desconocido," "On the Poet Coming of Age," "First Beating," and "Archeology" in *Touching the Fire: Fifteen Poets of Today's Latino Renaissance;* "Bird Ave" in *Floricanto Sí: A collection of Latina Poetry*, 1998; "Summer Ends Too Soon" and "Migration" in *Luna*, 1998; "Isla Mujeres" and "On the Poet Coming of Age" in *Under the Pomegranate Tree: Latino Erotica*, 1996; "Bird Ave," "Oda a las Gatas," & "Astro-No-Mia" in *Chicana Criticism, Chicana Creativity*, 1996; "On Childhood" in The Bloomsbury Review, 1997; "Liberty," "Tierra Y Libertad," "A Baldemar Gómez," and "Homing" in *Visiones*, 1995; "Ode a las Gatas" in *TumbleWords: Writers Reading the West*, 1995; "Archeology" and "First Beating" in *Many Mountains Moving*, 1994.

Some of the poems in "PLAY" first appeared in a rare limited edition of *Play* (MANGO Publications, 1999).

The author wishes to express her gratitude to The National Endowment of the Arts for a Creative Writing Fellowship in Poetry, The Lila Wallace - Readers Digest Fund for a LWRD Fund Award for Poetry, The Colorado Council on the Arts and Humanities for a Literary Arts Fellowship Grant, the University of Colorado at Boulder for a Dean's Grant from the School of Arts and Sciences, CMAS at the University of Houston for a Visiting Scholar Fellowship, The Xicanao Writers' Group, and all my students – without you this wouldn't be. Y gracias a toda la buena gente de Isla Mujeres, QR, MEXICO, y su gran poeta, Rafael Burgos Ríos. Gracias a la vida. Thanks, Javi, my Star. And many thanks, Bryce.

In memory of Rose, my mother,
who, upon watching me write five entire poems
in one day in my fifteenth year, said,
"You tell 'em, Lorna! And after you tell 'em,
you tell 'em who told you to tell 'em."

And the fire and the rose are one.

– T. S. Eliot

"How Far's the War?"

"How Far's the War?"

You Are

you are salty when I kiss
the sea calm in your skin / I hear clocks /
chiming the hours different from the hours
that we lived here / hours that bring me the bird

perched in your voice / the water bird /
the bird which lies on the floor of the sea / opening
little paths where the stars
can come down at night / so the day can begin /
all the days begin this way / with the stars coming down
to shelter the bones of the compañeros / to take
a lighted coal from a burning compañero /
a compañero's clear dream /

to go out / to star up again / to write on the night
"juan's compañeros hear the sounds the sun makes /
the sounds they make under the sun /
compañeros togethering / they fall silent in a solar way /"
the day begins
with a warm heart / it lights fires
in meditation / the elbow / the shadow
that opens its eyes in your sea

you are beloved by me and by the compañeros who lie in the south /
waiting for the stars each night / the adventure of the day /
a child spreading his white hair over you /
a woman passing my soul out around the world /
the compañeros let their angel fall like autumns /
on each little leaf they wrote an unknown heart /
from each little leaf a compañero will rise up
and tie up the stars so you will love me /

– Juan Gelman

For My Ancestors Adobed
in the Walls of the Santa Barbara Mission

after Phil Goldvarg

The bones that hold the holy.
Bones, grafted from bailing
and tar. The feathers
of a sleeker bird
resting in the nest.
The wry sense of autumn
calling like a winning smile.

The rapid fire. The wind
laid rest. The certainty
of servitude. The last ash
for the piki. Petals of a lost
desire. A woman's breast
releasing a flower of milk
on her dress. Buckskin bark
carpets the forests. Manzanita
swirls its own polish, her old bone
gleam. Her steady burn. The burl.

Bones weighed in at market.
The single bones, the married
bones with bands on bones.
Bones of a bonzai rectitude,
a fortitude of factories
on the horizon. Bones to raise
a Nation. An axe. An awl.

Bones stripped of their acorns.
Bones nipped from the grave.
Baskets of mourning
foreign to the settlers.
Baskets of bones
with rattlers inside.
Baskets of bones
with the teeth in hide.
Bounties of bones
with the people inside.

For every sale
there is a bone.
For every bone
there is a home
and a prayer
calling out the human heart,
chants on a drum
of human hide
with the bill of sale
still inside. And a brand
name still entails
a tag on the toe, a museum
label, a designer death
for you who were buried
with the names inside.

I say this peace, purple dove
of passion for you
who were robbed as bones.
For you who were stripped
of your meat. For you who were
worked to death grinding corn
at the metate you toted

for their feed, the sweet
smoke of age barely at your tail
when they packed you up for good
rebar for the reinforcement.

Oh, Savior of the Mission of Bones,
Oh, Designer Death for the Architect,
Pope of the Bones
and the sainted orders –
the sainted terrorists.

Bones that hold,
the Holy.

Amen
     d.

In the Waiting Room

A dead man, yellow margins
and a date, lamps and magazines,
rivulets of fire. It got dark,
the inside of a volcano. Over
people, photographs
full of ashes, 'round and 'round
a waiting room, an appointment
slung on a wire. Too long
to stop that nothing stranger,
a big black slush, the fifth
of falling, those awful similarities,
a different pair of hands.
Then, I was back in it, of falling off.
The room was bright. War,
a loud cold wait.

Coffee

I.

In Guatemala the black buzzard
has replaced the quetzal
as the national bird. The shadow
of a man glides across the countryside,
over the deforested plantations; a death
cross burnishes history into myth
as it scours the medicinal land into coffee;
burial mounds that could be sites
of unexcavated knowledge hold only
blasted feathers and the molding bones
of freedom. Golden epaulets glint
in the fluorescent offices, crystal
skulls shine in the eyes of the man
with the machete, within the site
of an AK-47. Under the rubble
of the ruling class, a human heart
beats in the palm, the tumba of ritual mercy
drums in the thunder clap, a hurricane wind
sounds the concha. In Quetzaltenango, foreign
interests plot the futures of Mayan hands
and Incan gold. While on Wall Street,
the black sludge of a people trickles through
cappuccino machines like hissing snakes.

II

Acteal. December 22, 1997. Bloodied
mud sucks the plastic sandals of a child,
velas gutter through the saged prayers
in the little church blasted through with
twenty-two splintered holes the size
of a baby's tender fists. Melon heads pop
and the hacking drum of a machete
meeting bone counts down the hours
of matanza. Somewhere, a telephone
rings off the hook. The Vicar of the Diocese
calls in twenty minute intervals. 140 federales
stand smoking in the twilight, at their feet,
the trampled harvest of peasants gleams
through the saturated leaves. Homero
Tovilla Cristiani picks up the phone: "I have
notified General Jorge Gamboa Solis. Everything
is under control. There is no massacre in Acteal."
He places the receiver again off the cradle
on the well-ordered desk. Meanwhile, a young
Tzotzil bloodies her knuckles scratching a hole
in the adobed wall of a cave feathered with Jaguar
fur where 14 women and children wait,
shivering in the dark. An infant picks up the call.
The first woman in line gazes into the coked-up eyes
of her assassin projecting his automatic weapon
into the ear of the whimpering baby at her breast.
500 years of history gets written in her eyes, as a Tzotzil
mother wedges her sleeping newborn into the hole.
She spits on the reddening dirt, and covers
her luz like a cat. Forty five pair of shoes
get lost in Acteal. Matted hair clings
to the coffee plants, each green leaf,

another listening ear; each red seed,
another eye, dislodged from its skull. I hear
nothing happened in Acteal. And if it did
no one knows who they were. The PRI
press machine stands on the ridge
of Destiny, staring Truth in the eye
as men lie to the cameras. Twenty yards
away, the survivors are speaking
the names of the men paid 600 dollars
American. Men with no families but a spoon
and a copa. Men with no names but the trademarks
emblazoned across their chests and on their running shoes.
I hear forty-five graves being dug today.
The women form a chain of hearts.
They have dried the earth baked with their tears.
Each one carries a red mud brick
from the killing floor where the people
were hacked into pieces the size of a bat.
Here, the "Bat People," Tzotziles, will
build a house for their dead, and pray.

III

Alonso Vázquez Gómez
María Luna Méndez
Rosa Vázquez Luna
Verónica Vázquez Luna
Mícaela Vázquez Luna
Juana Vázquez Luna
Juana Luna Vázquez
María Jímenez Luna
Susana Jímenez Luna
Miguel Jímenez Pérez
Marcela Luna Ruíz
Alejandro Luna Ruíz
Jaime Luna Ruíz
Regina Luna Pérez
Roselia Luna Pérez
Ignacio Pukuj Luna
Mícaela Pukuj Luna
Victorio Vázquez Gómez
Augustín Gómez Ruíz
Juana Pérez Pérez
Juan Carlos Luna Pérez
Marcela Vázquez Vázquez
Antonia Vázquez Vázquez
Lorenzo Gómez Pérez
Verónica Pérez Oyalte
Sebastian Gómez Pérez
Daniel Gómez Pérez
Pablina Hernández Vázquez
Rosela Gómez Hernández
Graciela Gómez Hernández
Guadalupe Gómez Hernández
María Ruíz Oyalte

Catalina Vázquez Pérez
Catalina Luna Ruíz
Manuela Paciencia Moreno
Margarito Gómez Paciencia
Rosa Gómez Pérez
Doida Ruíz Gómez
Augustín Ruíz Gómez
Rosa Pérez Pérez
Manuel Vázquez Pérez
Juana Vázquez Pérez
Josefa Vázquez Pérez
Marcela Capote Vázquez
Marcela Capote Ruíz

We are One Spirit, One Heart and One Mind.

IV

Marseilles. Summer of 1940.
In the Cafe Rue d' Bohéme, a poet,
Hans Sahl, sits waiting for someone
to buy him a cup of coffee in exchange
for witty repartee. He is a dead man.
His name has appeared on a list of German
refugees commanded to "Surrender on Demand."
He is convinced he will never leave France
except by cattle car. A compatriot tells him
an American was asking for him by name,
that "Varian Fry is now waiting for him at the
Hotel Splendide with money and an emergency
visa." He thinks the man is crazy or
it is a joke crueler than fate for a Jew.
He sits in the Cafe all day, writing his last poems
on the coffee splotched napkins. He writes:

Sprich

Not to lost causes present your heart.
Nor love those who cast you from their midst.
Forget dark visions your dreams impart.
Forget the hand that pushed you into emptiness.

Let not phantom sounds tear you apart
That yesterday's world brings to your ear.
Not to lost causes present your heart.
Guard yourself until your hour's here.

He empties the bitter cups of coffee, knowing
they are the last he will ever taste in unoccupied

France. That fall, he sits in a Greenwich Village cafe, the cooling coffee sweetened with the blood of the funny little man who brushed in the stamp on his forged exit visa. He vows to spend the rest of his days praising the man who defied the orders of nations, Nazis, industry, collaborators, gendarmes, and the United States Consulate.

"Sprich" was copied from a napkin on display in the Varian Fry exhibit at the National Holocaust Museum.

V

Work is the refuge of sadness.
"Only when we remember does sadness
overcome us and we cry. It's better
to just keep busy," says María Ruíz.
The women knead the masa under the heels
of their hands, cupping the balls of cornmeal
pocked with a few black beans. They pat
the bolas into palm-sized portions: golden
ears of corn, black eyes of frijol, red tongues
of chili. On December 23rd there is laughter
in Polhó. The señoritas giggle at the gringo's
questions. "Qué tiene? Qué tiene?" Meaning,
What is inside this humble feast they are
preparing for the ones who have come with
provisions and witness? "What's the matter?"
"Qué tiene?" The gringo insists. They smile,
a coy reply. "Nada." Nada. There is nothing
in Acteal. The federales have stolen the well-packed
sacks of coffee, a year's hard labor. They have
torn-up the clothing, peed on the grain, slaughtered
the animals, taken radios, cooking pots, weaving,
looms. The same soldiers who shit in the kitchen
now sport yellow arm bands reading Labor Social.
Work is the refuge of sadness.
Work is more than the sum of a job.
"We need to finish off the seed!"
Mícaela heard them shout.
She had been praying in the chapel since six.
At eleven she heard the gunfire start.
Men and women were on their knees.
Some stood up and began to run. Some fell
in the chapel. The only way out was the steep

embankment. Her mother took her by the hand
and carried the two youngest. The bullet
entered her mother's back. They were found
by the children's cries. First they shot her
mother, then the babies. She made no sound
under her mother's cooling huipil. "Diego,
Antonio y Pedro. More than fifty from Los Chorros,
Pechiquíl, La Esperanza, Acteal. They were dressed
in black. The ones in charge had military uniforms."
She testifies to the National Human Rights Commission.
She testifies to anyone who works to listen. How they
stripped the dead women and sliced their breasts,
forced sticks between their legs, opened the wombs,
passing the fetuses from machete to machete. . . .
Where once she worked to silence her siblings,
at 11, Mícaela's work is to be the mouth
of a people. Behind each of the names
is a life, lost between the reporter's lines
and the photograph's caption.

VI

"No more genocide in my name. . . ."
A young girl in trenzas sings outside
The Mexican Consulate in Denver.
"Go back to where you came from!"
shouts a car of gringos speeding down
memory lane, and is nearly drowned out
by the ritual drums and the Native chants.
First World faces sing out above the placards
like severed heads or scalps. "No more Genocide . . ."
. . . in Guatemala, Colombia, El Salvador, Chile,
Sand Creek, Wounded Knee. . . . Not with arms.
Not with training. Not with money. No more
of my tax dollars that buys the man who drives
the Humvee that transports the soldier who shoots
the weapon that blinds the toddler, that enters the heart
of Guadalupe López Méndez who dies in Ocosingo
asserting her civil rights. No more Genocide
in my name. We shall not overcome. We shall fight
this way forever. Estas son mis armas:
la computadora, el video, la pluma.
La plumage de justicia hangs from the broken
arrows of palabras breaking the media block
of Truth and Consequences of Free Trade Agreements.
Horrific to read, to imagine, to know, to tell –
but the only end to bullets for profit is knowledge –
knowledge that will not appear wedged between
commercials for Taster's Choice and
Nobody Doesn't Like Sara Lee like the living body of
an indigenous child found two days after massacre
in a bullet-ridden cave. Is this any way to fight
a drug war? Coffee, sugar, chocolate,

cattle.... "N ... É ... S ... T ... L ... E ... S ...
Néstles makes the very best ... MUR ... DER!"
310 kilos of cocaine are found in Mazatán,
the municipality where the governor, Julio César
Ruíz Ferro, has two large mansions, a ranch
with a hundred hectare banana plantation and,
is building a luxury hotel with 100 suites, underground
parking, boat dock, restaurant, bar and disco.
Revenue from taxing an impoverished indigenous
population was good this year. Meanwhile,
the Mexican Red Cross sends contaminated
and expired drugs to the thousands of refugees
dying of exposure, pneumonia, and other infections
in the frigid mountains. "Néstles makes the very best ...
MUR ... DER!" 15 billion served, ground flesh
for the masses. I will grind Zapatista coffee
with the tongues of witness. I will wear
the huipil and honor the mothers. I will write
the dark into dawn. I will sit in the offices,
shut down the lying dog press, picket
the congress into action. I will not bank
with assassins. I will buy crafts, not Kraft,
Néstles, Proctor & Gamble, McDonald's, Sara Lee....
I will fight this way forever. Estas son mis armas:
la computadora, el video, la pluma.
"A culture isn't vanquished until the hearts
of its mothers are lying on the ground."
I will fight this way forever: I will say.
I will fight this way forever: I will pay.
I will fight this way forever: I will pray.
Amen. Y Con Safos.

El Cinco de Mayo, 1998

Bananas

for Indrek

I

In Estonia, Indrek is taking his children
to the Dollar Market to look at bananas.
He wants them to know about the presence of fruit,
about globes of light tart to the tongue, about the
twang of tangelos, the cloth of persimmons,
the dull little mons of kiwi. There is not a chance
for a taste where rubles are scarce and dollars, harder.
Even beef is doled out welfare-thin on Saturday's platter.
They light the few candles not reserved for the dead,
and try not to think of the small bites of the coming winter,
irradiated fields or the diminished catch in the fisherman's
net. They tell of bananas yellow as daffodils. And mango –
which tastes as if the whole world came out from her womb.

II

Colombia, 1928, bananas rot in the fields.
A strip of lost villages between railyard
and cemetery. The United Fruit Company
train, a yellow painted slug, eats
up the swamps and jungle. Campesinos
replace Indians who are a dream and a rubble
of bloody stones hacked into coffins: malaria,
tuberculosis, cholera, machetes of the jefes.
They become like the empty carts that shatter
the landscape. Their hands, no longer pulling green
teats from the trees, now twist into death, into silence
and obedience. They wait in Aracataca, poised
as statues between hemispheres. They would rather
be tilling their plots for black beans. They would
rather grow wings and rise as pericos – parrots, poets,
clowns – a word which means all this, pericos, those
messengers from Mictlán, the underworld, where ancestors
of the slain arise with the vengeance of Tláloc. A stench
permeates the wind as bananas, black on the stumps, char
into odor. The murdered Mestizos have long been cleared
and begin their new duties as fertilizer for the plantations.
Feathers fall over the newly spaded soil: turquoise,
scarlet, azure, quetzal, and yellow litters
the graves with the gold claws of bananas.

III

Dear I,
The 3' x 6' boxes in front of the hippie
market in Boulder are radiant with marigolds, some
with heads as big as my Indian face. They signify
death to me, as it is Labor Day and already
I am making up the guest list for my Día de los Muertos
altár. I'll need maravillas so this year I plant caléndulas
for blooming through snow that will fall before November.
I am shopping for "no-spray" bananas. I forego
the Dole and Chiquita, that name that always made me
blush for being christened with that title. But now
I am only a little small, though still brown enough
for the – Where are you from? Probably my ancestors
planted a placenta here as well as on my Califas coast
where alien shellfish replaced native mussels,
clams and oysters in 1886. I'm from
the 21st Century, I tell them, and feel
rude for it – when all I desire
is bananas without pesticides. They're smaller
than plantains which are green outside and firm
and golden when sliced. Fried in butter
they turn yellow as over-ripe fruit. And sweet.
I ask the produce manager how to crate and
pack bananas to Estonia. She glares at me
suspiciously: You can't do that. I know.
There must be some law. You might spread
diseases. They would arrive as mush, anyway.
I am thinking of children in Estonia with
no fried plátanos to eat with their fish as
the Blond turns away, still without shedding
a smile at me – me, Hija del Sol, Earth's Daughter, lover
of bananas. I buy up Baltic wheat. I buy up organic
bananas, butter y canela. I ship
banana bread.

IV

At Big Mountain uranium
sings through the dreams of the people.
Women dress in glowing symmetries, sheep
clouds gather below the bluffs, sundown
sandstone blooms in four corners. Smell of sage
penetrates as state tractors with chains trawl the resisting
plants, gouging anew the tribal borders, uprooting
all in their path like Amazonian ants, breaking
the hearts of the widows. Elders and children
cut the fences again and again as wind whips
the waist of ancient rock. Sheep nip across
centuries in the people's blood, and are carried
off by Federal choppers waiting in the canyon
with orders and slings. A long winter, little wool
to spin, medicine lost in the desecration of the desert.
Old women weep as the camera rolls on the dark
side of conquest. Encounter rerun. Uranium. 1992.

V

I worry about winter in a place
I've never been, about exiles in their
homeland gathered around a fire,
about the slavery of substance and
gruel: *Will there be enough to eat?*
Will there be enough to feed? And
they dream of beaches and pies, hemispheres
of soft fruit found only in the heat of the planet.
Sugar cane seeks out tropics; and dictates
a Resolution to stun the tongues of those
who can afford to pay: imported plums, bullets,
black caviar large as peas, smoked meats
the color of Southern lynchings, what we don't
discuss in letters. You are out of work.
Not many jobs today for high physicists
in Estonia, you say. Poetry, though, is food
for the soul. And bread? What is cake before
corn and the potato? Before the encounter
of animals, women and wheat? Stocks, high
these days in survival products: 500 years later tomato
size tumors bloom in the necks of the pickers.
On my coast, Diablo dominates the golden hills,
the faultlines. On ancestral land, Vandenberg shoots
nuclear payloads to Kwajalein, a Pacific atoll, where 68%
of all infants are born amphibian or anemones. But poetry
is for the soul. I speak of spirit, the yellow seed
in air as life is the seed in water, and the poetry
of Improbability, the magic in the Movement
of quarks and sunlight, the subtle basketry
of hadrons and neutrinos of color, how what you do
is what you get – bananas or worry.
What do you say? Your friend,

a Chicana poet

Portrait of a Little Boy
Feeding a Stray in Sarajevo

The kitten isn't interested in bread;
you can tell from its lip it's purring.
She is looking at the boy, the expression
of his intent. He is on a mission: he is feeding
the poor. He squats in the crevice of the cave
where the shell has landed on, but not destroyed,
the busy orphanage. His black sneakers
bear a hole the shape of the cracked cornerstone
as if his right little toe were on a journey of its own,
freed from the master foot. He could be
an altar boy, lighting the candles, striking
the chest, swinging the forbidden religious
sap. But he's not. He's content, for the time,
coaxing the cat with a yellow morsel the size of
a severed thumb. It could be chicken. But the cat
isn't interested in chicken. She sits, shabby, on
her haunches like the boy. Her white fists knead
the rubble as if this mother were wearing a political
shirt with the slogan, unreadable in this moment.
His outstretched arm on the knee, balanced
as a circus trainer, disciplined. As orphan
and stray gaze into each other's eyes like
dance partners, trapeze artists, madonna
and child, eating at the eons between beast
and civil society with the universal tongue.

At the Fishhouse

Over and over, that black old knife,
that better judgment laid horizontally,
a dark purple brown, completely rusted,
suspended in total immersion,
that cold, dank and deep
spilling over, considering an ancient
decline, a heavy surface,
suspended, almost worn away.
A heart would burn as if waiting
for Christmas. Free above the
world. If you should dip your hand in
you would associate with shadows.

"How to Explain Paintings to a Dead Hare"

a love sonnet for Joseph Beuys

Take a bit of copper between your teeth.
Bite down hard while pressing the first two
Fingertips of each hand firmly into wood.
A writing desk is good. Your kitchen table, better.

Visualize the Cross and Crucifixion.
Notice color. Don't think of mass graves.
Relax. Let go the metal. Discard.
In the case of a penny, spend.

Pour a glass of orange juice.*
Hold the cold mouthful. Rinse the first
Taste of fresh blood from the tongue.
Spit. Drink the rest of the glass.

Bring it to the gaslight.
Imagine your reflection in the bristling fat.

* *bear the fruit/ of unpoisoned trees/ & bless the bees*

Ten One-Line Poems to America

1.

America, you dream into the foxhole of a wounded heart.

2.

America, you suckle on the scars of war.

3.

America, peace is a many tendered thing.

4.

America, you are the path cut throughout.

5.

America, grief is a many splintered thing.

6.

America, death is a global village.

7.

America, we are the song waiting to be sung.

8.

America, don't build me a country to mourn.

9.

America, too much freedom is just enough.

10.

America, you are the poem waiting to happen.

For Love, for Sept. 11

When it broke – a fine-haired
line of tarnished foil before the growling weight
of glass and fire, crisp with blood,
venerable and homely like full-blown roses,
falling petals, rosettes of rust,
weaponlike, and still attached –

they didn't fight.
They hadn't fought at all.
Victory spread a rainbow
of oil, thwarted and sun-cracked.
The morning, like an oarlock on a string,
the tipping far longer. The steel
hung in strips like ancient wallpaper
lost through ages. The rented
cubicles, the strain of lights,
all that can cut so badly,
the big bones and the little bones
packed in like feathers.
I find them on a summer's night
in mind like a magician's sleeve,
their narrow piercing guesses are
whatever you believe.

9/11/03

"We Have a Country of Words"

after Mahmoud Darwish, 9-12-01

a country you carry in your pocket
airport to airport, a country
that exists for you in remembered
fragrance, an expired stamp, now the seal
of blood embossed upon someone's
sunstruck pavement. Who owns
this property? Who owns the right
to no way out but a busted window
a hundred flights up? Who owns the key
to Heaven's Gate? Did it open?

I open the newspaper, my computer,
an account, and need to account for all
the terror in the world, in crossing
the street with my child this morning:
my Indian head, my Palestinian shroud.
With what do we pay? For what
attention? I want to draw its shape
scattered in files and surprises . . .
flying on shrapnel and bird's wings . . .
trapped between the dagger and the wind.
I want to draw your shape
to find my shape in yours. . . .

And what if the source
of death is not the dagger
or the lie, but both?
Buried deep in the human rubble.

Closer to God
than thee.

9:50 a.m.

We may be bits of flesh
blown asunder by a changling wind
but this blast of paper lasts – our change.

12:03 p.m.

No. I won't stand silent.
I won't fly a flag
I can't afford to buy.
I go out into the garden
and plant my expired seed.

American Haiku

Squirrels in my back
yard are never there
when I hold the hose.

Coca Cola

Black blood of imperialism,
sed de las selvas, distilled, watered
down, mesclado, sweet and
fermented as revenge. Little
volcanos of gas, uprisings
of air, a revolution waiting
to happen.

Blood: Black Burned Oil of the Race

That which happened in the Temple
Of Oil happens everywhere.
All enchanted. All drunk from the
Other – all for nothing, for
No one. For peace – the other side,
Way of Gold: all for all. Nothing
For one, the few with mountains of
Everything: the blood; birds, dead from
The poverty; the shadow of
Soul; the race, a burned bone, the bone

Stripped of desire, the bone dry
From witness; hand in the empty
Air and full of salutations
For life. Look. All that is! All that is
Burning. And breaking like so many
Hearts. Listen! You with the fist of
Flesh and Brotherhood. Open it,
Already you play the guitar of
Resistence, the power of all.
Power of nothing. Power of zero.

Power of the water drop by
Drop and side by side, hand to fist
To Sister, Brother. They love those
Who love nothing. Buy it! Nothing
Made from nothing more than hunger
And the blows of desperation
Or the wee drops of brains raining

On the streets and black windows,
Small mirrors from the street children,
black depleted uranium

Deleted in this final Book
Of Hope – basket of hope, woven
Weaving of love, Contra-Buyer,
Of root and *"NO!"*

Sangre: Petról Negro de la Raza 'Humada

Lo que pasó en el Templo
Del Petról pasa por todo
Todos encantados, todos
Borachos del Otro – todo

Para nada, para nadie.
Por la paz el otro lado,
Camino del Oro: todo
para todo. Nada para

Uno, lo poco con montón
De todo: la sangre, aves
Muertos de la pobreza, la
Sombra del alma, la raza,

Hueso quebrado, el hueso
Desnudo del deseo, el
Hueso seco del testigo –
Mano al aire vacio

Y lleno de saludos por
Vida. Mira. ¡Todo lo que es!
¡Todo lo que está quemando!
Y quebrando como tantos

Corazones. ¡Oyé! Tú
Con la mano de carne y
Carnalismo: Ábrelo, ya
Tocas en la guitarra de

Resisténcia, el poder
De todo. Poder de nada.
Poder de zéro. Poder del
Agua gota a gota y

Lado a lado, mano a
'Mano, 'Mano. Aman los que
No aman nada. Cómprala
Nada hecho por nada mas

Que el hambre y los golpes
De la desperación o
Las gotitas de cerebros
Lluviando por las calles y

Ventanas negras, espejos
Pequeños de los niños de
La calle como uranio
"Depleted." Deleted in this

Final chapter of Hope, woven
Basket de la esperanza
Tejido del Amor, Contra-
Comprador, de raíz y *¡NO!*

Murder

they'll have to kill us first
that should be a given
they will have to take us
each one of us
clamp our wet mouths shut
with their star-grinned hand
full of lies

or they have to kill us

like they kill us in their uniforms
(we all know that)
the way they take us when we're young
and play Russian Roulette with our skulls
but this
is not a poem about that
this is a poem
about writing poems

about the state
of writing poems
in this state when the state
dons uniforms
to shoot us in the head
and then denies it
with good reason
and reasons
justified by arms

let me explicate first
before you get the idea that this is rhetoric
I once lived down the street
from the Treviños
whose son/brother/uncle/grandson
Danny Treviño was shot pointblank
in the back of the head
by the badges whose reason
was that Danny was drunk
(a minor passed-out on the floor of his car)

now if I were to write a poem
about the death of Danny Treviño
I would not use rhetorical devises
I would wield the filigree of images
I learned to use in order to write fine poetry
I would write a poem about how
tight the shot rang out that night
I could hear it from my mama's house
as clear as I could hear the trains
and then I would go on to say
just how much those trains meant to me
and how they were symbolic
of the masculine death machine

but this is not that kind of poem
this is a poem about the act of writing
poems
in an extreme State

and I call it
MURDER

Corky's First Elegy

"He is somewhere down
amid the withered
sedge and alder bushes there
by the water's edge, but where?
From that quarter his shrill blast
sounded, but he is silent, and
a kingdom will not buy it again."

– from The Journal of Henry David Thoreau
9 April, 1856

Corky's Next Elegy

a kingdom – blast
withered amid the Bushes
silent sounded
shrill
somewhere down
that quarter by the water's edge
there, but where?

from his – a journal, and an April
will not buy it again

– 13 de abril
he has passed on a portal day, 13 Ahau

42

After the Wake

for Ed Dorn

Some things I don't confess
to know. How a dead man
gets up out of bed, the Blue Bonnets
of Texas all over his gown, how stark
the room he wakes from, and summons you
to talk. I forgot what he said.
He did look dead, though later
said he was just resting. The rest
was trees, some kind of Ash; I aspire
to know them, what landscape was this,
like a neutron explosion – nothing left but the leaves,
nothing standing, no stone that wasn't formed
by the sea. No corners. Smashed.

Untitled

Open the hand that racks
cinder from a nesting of hovels, the cardboard
city where bread is never warm and
memory lines the alleys in a windsuit of denim.
After the winter of order, the black patrol
breaks the camp with billy clubs and bins, a
music of sirens and silence punctuate
the coffin refrain of hunger.
Despair the hand as you would
a stone in the border, and remove it.

On Why I Boycotted Cinco de Mayo

Coors

The News

3 crossburnings
3 bodies in a swollen river

3 crossburnings
3 bodies bloating in a river

3 crossburnings
3 little girls naked in the river

3 crossburnings
3 dirty girls terrorizing a river

3 crossburnings
3 barreling boys a-slippin' in the river

3 crossburnings
3 stripped sisters clogging up a river

3 crossburnings
3 barreling brothers a-slippin' in moon river

3 crossburnings
2 brothers, and another

found dead in a frigid river
officials investigate

and the battle
..............................looms

3 crossburnings
2 brothers, and another

3 crossburnings
3 unidentified bodies left drowned in a river

3 crossburnings
officials investigate

and the battle
..............................looms

3 crossburnings
3 dark-haired girls

found dead in a desert
2 brothers, and another

3 forms of Truth
found dead in a frigid river

officials investigate
and the battle

..............................looms

On Columbus Day

for Russell Means

I would teach this day,
bind them to a presence
and death. Talk about what it means
to make sense, to catch
one's breath and lasso
da Vinci's star to your chest –
"He turns not back
who is bound to a star."

I heard this today
in the killer magpies,
a fray of desire
for meat, for prey.

Talk about a Nation
of Four Corners, summit
of the heart, the stone
pulling through, a concentric
concentration, a talking
to Infinity: The Constitution
of a Star of Unity
in the Iroquois
Confederacy.

Talk about what we need
more of – some dangling
change, some synergy;
more love, more time to do it,
more Justice, more Virtue,

Fortitude, Prudence,
and Temperance – the Cardinal
Directions.

I heard it say,
"We are our children's past,
and our heart's can affect
infinity . . . a responsibility."
Our hearts can beat
for eternity.

---

* *"He turns not back who is bound to a star." From a speech by Russell Means at the All Nations March, Denver, 10/03.*

Chaya: V

The frigate doesn't always get
her fish. She dives. She plunges
in, her heart in her head. All of the morter
in her wings, aloft; alive with the bounty
of best. Again.

We earned this battle. History,
forgotten four times over, the foreigner
always wins. The vanquished concedes
the sugar. We've given all we got.
Now we are the receivers, the perceivers
feeling our way past destiny.
What we are is a bitten fruit
gazing into the sacrifice
of the sun; the rotations of the hemispheres
known to us a millenia before
NASA. We receive the data of the dead
on the butterflies flight – those tourists
to the nine unknowns, the first explorers
stitching the continents back into the memory of when
they were one vast turtle's back.
Perceivers of the nine dimensions
– what isn't said in words.

You burned the books
so you wouldn't know.
We burned the books
so you wouldn't take
more. More of the same,
the pillage and rape

of the deepest dark, the grand
debauch in another country, on
another tongue, the conquering
of the mind. I didn't say
you did this. I say
this is history. It is not
the song.

We sing in our sleep, wake
remembering – how not to kill
for the shape of the Other's fears,
how to feed the mouths that
say us. Speak to me not of dreams,
but of the songs you hear in your head,
the Mother Tongue lapping at the banks
of worlds. The New World crumbling
in on ourselves, all the towers imploding,
the twin desires caving in to empathic
imagination. We are how we imagine
the other to be. Let us be
happy in the pursuit of peace. Free
to stand for as long as we want
without some other saying,
"No! You can't stand here.
This is mine,"
without imagining
another country
same as the rest.

On Saving Hans Bethe (Californium: III)

I was holding the hand of Hiroshima,
I was palming the damaged workers
in the holes of a nuclear hell.
I was holding a frail nation
up by the arm, propping
aristocracy up by the delicate
wrist. My covetous place
finally, firmly in lockstep
with the withered Age
of Reason. Here,
take my hand,
talk of peace,
the Big Bang
and the Final Dis-
                    solution.
I have only dishwater to waste,
what we do with our hands & heart,
as we take a serious trajectory
through a vaguing past
and the fairied future,
as we weave in slo-mo
through the impatient face
of now in its shimmering
vehicles. Let it wait.
Let me clutch the hand that
drove us into space. Let me
guide the calculation of the race
to his place of rest, into
the formula of fusion and the
fission of our final desti-
nation. Wait.

Atole

for Edward Long

You were ground down
in the molcajete, spiced
grit with a chocolate soul.
Homeless as a shucked
kernel, expelled by the
lover's hand. Sand and
pepper, unshaven on your chin.
Calloused wisdom of a fool.
City worker, grimy digger,
how the streets and courts
chewed your cardboard shoes
to shame. But you sweetened
my mañanas, fed me poetry
from your gruel.

From the Bus to E.L.
at Atascadero State Hospital

for Juan Cuellar

Fall. Peppercorns
rouge into salmon roe.
The finished hills, blonde
in Califas, get crew cuts
as cattle butch the hip grass
into flat-tops. Five o'clock
shadows singe and vanquish
without felling the scrub oaks
and manzanita snarls. Dusted
summer squash laze on the gone
lawns, ready pumpkins in the fields,
bright as plastic and faceless, their time
up, evident as flaring matches in The Hole.
There's a town coming on. It shows
in the Greyhound windows, the mooned
mounds instantly green – fence
and civilize.
                    They sat you
here, where you stuck
like a poisoned dart
between the Idler Bar
and the Mud Hole Mini Mart.
Small wonder, vato, you
envisioned your Jupiterscapes
here in these Martianed landings. What
messages they blew to this world, the seeds
of something generative.

Someday, you said, they would
blow us both away.
                   There was a code
to be read in the nothing of an empty page.
There was a plan to the shambles
of sage on the rocks or the bumbling
kooks on the blocked streets,
the nothing of a stranger
who refuses to give, the nothing
of a television mouthing
nothing to a nothing house full
of nothing, like on the morning they locked
you up for good.
                  You were here, Ed,
and there is nothing here. Moonscapes,
desert wastes. As it is, in this light,
the eyes read but register nothing: cables
and telephone trees, white fences, the immovable
air vanishing on the nude hips of comatose women.
Is this what you saw? Nothing
in the hedges, the chopped ends, the panicking
roads where nothing is distanced
between ourselves and an abundance
of nowhere.
             The institutions of our lives
embed themselves in the shallows like the clumped
row houses of Camp Roberts, the wooden graves
of the suicidal dead or the wars where
they laid you to rest, resisting.
You could have gone on
to King City or the Temple
                       of Angels. Instead,
you were here where the wounded
blackbirds warble jazz to a crazed wind,

where the dusk is as pure and inimical
as law, devious as treaties, a substance
fills the night, the absence of light,
with whatever we imagine.
Think of it, spacetrips, vato
loco of the stars, this is what you get
in this life, the lockdown
of nothing.

BIRD AVE

BIRD AVE

I sing to you to feel the dream
Who would I be if I didn't sing?
For half a chance you spare nothing –
A tethered bird to a tethered cage.

But don't forget about the factory
I don't expect this ride to always be
Can I give them what they want to see?
Let me do it twice – the second time for me.

– Ferron
from "Shadows on a Dime"

BIRD AVE

life on Bird
was tough
Cat-eyes
me and Mousie
estrolándonos y
marchando
con missions
man I can't get no
satisfaction
in and out las
baby baby baby
oooOooOoo
baby baby
hits all summer

we wore tease
tight skirts
tough teased hair
talked tough
rhymes
developed
una re-puta-
ción for the toughest
burns on Horseshoe

tough
from Memorial Day
to our Labor Day
weekend
we had the key

to the drug locker
of our own developing
temples
highest kites in the district
favors all over town
and we owed
nobody shit

Cat-eyes was beautiful
Mouse made up wizard holds
nobody over 4 11 could contain her
except me – the connection
we always had it
we scored
when we wanted
plus we were *eth-i-cal*

essssahhh Mouse goes
at that first initiation
you gotta understand
about Ethics
she had it then
all total control
banging my head on
the blacktop for effect
you flacafeaface
got Ethics
and she gave me
one of those mouse
grins and squeezed
lemon crap
out of my cheeks
before letting me up
all righteous
rage

sin class   ni pomp
and circumstance
we were better
than military
beauty   brains & brass
we were the Trinity
that invented it
the model Rambos
I could'a killed her
easy
she knew it
we'd kill it
in ourselves
eventually

we knew it all
the code and the symbology
the poetics and the order
of place and gesture
we were honed for the killing
primed for the time
our ganga de camelias
y rosárias would burst
we tended that bust
cultivated it
blistered it
hitched ourselves
up to its hearse
and made up Bird
on the reins
of some wild ride
from the tracks to
Willow Glen and back
we were running

our own private
miracle mile
man
it was tough
with Cat-Eyes
on the corner
buttering 'em up
all stupid and blind
me and Mouse
always ready
to take advantage
of a relevant situation

Don't Fuck With Us
our motto
We're Here to Serve
the ruse
Listen   Watch
Be Silent
was the Conquest's
hidden code

man
it was tough
to know it all
and we haven't
learned anything
since

Oda a las Gatas

a Bird, Tiny, Mousie, Grumpy, Cat-Eyes,
Flaca, Sleepy, Princess y Betty la Boop

We were nine lives, cat claws plunged in
the caterwauling of la llorona and the crying saints.

We believed in witches, wild cards, jokers
and the tricksters who lived without it.

Disciples of the pride, we preyed on Furies' wings.
We lied. We stole the heart's desire. We never

got a cent, but feral, flew to another side
of glory. We came – this close to dying,

we gunned the engines of our grief – and gained.
Taught to live from hand to mouth, the moratorium

of our lives began at blood's first quickening.
Given to the beck and call so fast, we primed

our lives that instant when we slipped into the gap
between child and man – and slave. We chose

to stay, tough in the fist of our father's
mercy. No face cards in our deck, we dealt

the devil back his hand, we scorched the virgin
from our breasts, as the sweat of heat upon us

did not free us, but did not bind us either.
We had the power then, between three worlds,

to fuse our bruja pack, our pact to faith, not
in our futures but, in a present we could fix within

the diamond decks minted in our carboned eyes.
We were crystalline runaway rucas on the prowl:

edge of night in our glassy throats, cut of class
in flyaway manes, the blood of oils on our slapped

cheeks and with bit lips we smiled to
circling owls. No angels, no novenas, no past

spirits that we recognized, nobody's business
what we did, we know we earned our freedom,

and we did.

Pachucando

that's
what girls
did in
the barrio
to get
their 15
minutes
of fame
shoot out the lights
cut the hoses
walk the fence
get 'simmons
nuts
blood
oranges
in winter
plums
figs
in the fall
we formed
our own assaults
beat down
the beggars
called out
the maddogs
jammed up
the malls
teamwork

we badgered
up the will
we stole
our souls
from demons
won
face
saved
no dis
grace
grace
followed us
to bed
every night
on the prayers
de las angeles
late at night
the tongues
we buried
in our mothers'
tombs
calling
us out
like lemmings
painted lemurs
worried
gypsies
santeras
de la noche
salserando
through
the glassed
in streets

our smoking
copals
of marlboro
100s
flashing
in a burst
of lived air
cool
we were cold
fish eyes
ice skinned
grapes
fragrant
muy coiffed
and dressed
to kill
dry
as aged
lemon seeds
scattered
among the
crabby
drunks
our fathers
Lears
falling
upon
the empty
stage
made pitch
black
by our
shot-out
lights

Astro-no-mía

for Women in Science

The closest we ever got to Science
was the stars. Like the Big Dipper
ladling hundreds of thousands
of beans and diamonds for some Greeks
long ago when law was a story
of chased women set in the sky:
Diana, Daphne, Juno, Pleiades –
las hermanas siete: daughters, captives
of Atlas punished by Orion –
Coronis corded for infidelity,
and the children (the children) changed
into trees, bears, scared into stars.
We wished ourselves into that sky,
held our breath and stopped dreaming,
stopped stories, our hearts and escalated
up into that ash-trip to heaven – seven
smoked rings of escape from the chase.
Y nada. Punto. We were never stars.
Our mothers would call. The fathers
of fate, heavy like mercury, would trash
our stomachs back into wombs. Cold.
We'd rollercoaster back down to the earth,
to the night before school, before
failed examinations y *el otro*
which is much harder to describe.
Study? Sure. We studied hard.
But all I could remember was that man,
Orion, helplessly shooting his shaft
into my lit house from the bow.
¿Y Yo? Hay bow. Y ya me voy.

73

Summer Ends Too Soon

was the last she said. Beautiful
María, Ave María. María dodging
father's fists – and his. María praying
under the table. María crooning pain
songs in the bathroom. María combing
his sludge out of her hair. María
serving masters. Seventeen year
old María. María: Your Lady
of the Kept Secret. María dancing
to his temper. María washing
her panties in the toilet. Two
days after graduation, María
swaying from the limb. María:
sweet purple fruit of his sin.
Ave María.

Tasco

A woman carved her grief
into glittering rock, the stone
broke open a cloud mass and
water tore the paths to the church.
A basket of bread wept
on the table. A window
of breath disturbed the air
between the white-washed walls
as it opened, thrown wide
with the force of a punch.
A silence greened slow as summer,
moistened, fell apart, dissolved
into mud. She has thumbed the welt,
heard the cat wails within it as black
sweat pearls up the shaft. Here,
few hands grow tender that work
the mountains, extracting fossilized
tears from the refuse
of the mine.

The Barking Dogs of Mexico

All night they bay and snarl,
cut the air with salivating fangs.
These scabby browns and
salted skinny black dogs
are meek and resigned in the sun.
They obey, they acquiesce. They
scat with a kick or a spit.
They steal eggs from scratching
hens, crusts of bread from
between the road stones; but
sunset – they stretch, unfurl,
flex and pack. In the blanket
of nightfall they roam the calles,
take back the life that empties
from their ribs. And bite.

Agua Profunda

He says: This is where the women lay,
their final resting nest – sunk to the bottom-
less realm of the cenote, weighted with coral
and jade in the killing fields of beauty.
Where young men give their heads, the women
sacrifice breath: speech, their seed in water.
Rain is sperm, is poem, is storm, is accord,
is fertility, and life, in the language of the glyphs.
The serpent: bringer of oceans and venom.
But what if they slipped – cracking clothes on
the dull lime stones, what if they tumbled while
bathing, or cramped and went under, into silence
and speech, their final poem del agua profunda?

A Baldemar Gomez

(1955-74)

Baldemar, I never knew you.
This is why you are so easy
to talk to. Vén acá. Come
sit down. Take off that pain
mask. Sit as you were then,
in front of my plain pine desk.
Now that you are dead I am always
behind you. You, who murdered
your mother's heart for love, bitch
verses snarling up your dreams:
Her eyes were apricots, green
in March, and breasts like white
air. . . . Tonto, Baboso, dead of love
and La Gabacha didn't even deserve you.

Poet with the Lorca look and Pablo's
invisible cape, now it's come to this:
you're in the philosopher's noose. Now
you finger the robes of illumination; your sin,
a thing of the earth, what bloodied your ears
that first term at Yale, what played, mumblety-
pegged through your notebook pages: the war,
La Raza, locura in the barrio. De véras.
Your ghost hangs in the moonlight, cracking
above Hegel y San José where some girls scented,
and some accepted, your Chicano poetry, your
European stance, your tethered ways
to a dark romance with suicide.

Whore

You swore you were a virgin,
wove your hair into an empty nest,
wound your sorrow on your finger,
wound your silver strands into a golden
ring. You roared in a solitary
circle, soared in a sudden
dusk, came to light lit up
and bandied, candy in the hand
of the artful dodger, randy
along the way to a home with
a broken steeple. Wholly
rolling in the mill of bad will,
and hardened into a state
of lead the color of you
shot, dead.

Black and Blue

The velvet underground of that
first kiss. The awakening slap
of his sole. The tennis shoe skid
of a knee rising to her crotch.
The silk rope of hair in his fist.
The wet aroma of the drizzling rain;
how the blacktop survives the cracked
heat, how the clanking chains of the
tether tell, how an absentee bell
blairs away, and the tardiness checks
off another calendar day, the missed
period, the failing grade; and a lifetime
in black and blue invades.

Cheap Shot

There were no cheap shots
in the barrio, only hotshots
cruising by ride or by mouth.
Eh, what a burn, esa! On a
summer day, blacktop oozing
a mucky cannery sweat, smog,
a babyshit beige on the horizon.
Burned you good, Bug Eyes,
Moco Mouth. How much
it costs – to be. The question
of how much freedom
in the wit, a word,
a put-down/bring-you-up.
No change
expected.

Prom

She never did go to the prom.
1972, and all her friends
were showing up in drag
and a tuxedo was just
too many cents. So they spent
the night, and part of the next,
in the bleachers – ripped
aluminum steps, cold beer
on their backs, the horizon
just above a smoked-up future,
the great boiler of the moon
like a cardboard marquis
before the factory chugging out
their dream with the smell of potato
chips and burnt crayolas.

Crackling Fingers

We wove our hearts with our
hands, arms, clasps, head
strong alley-cat survivals
at our breaking tip. We took
no tips. We got our pay.
We got advanced. We were too
advanced. Quixotic
to the touch, to the
metallic hot
on all that bar, too much
tongue, all that
cool, and gone to waste.
They would hold our waists
on those wasted ways
to wit, with crackling fingers,
with lips of dun.

California Plum

*for Nathan Trujillo, discovered frozen to death
in a public restroom in Boulder, Colorado,
Feb. 3, 1992, and identified only as "a derelict."*

I suppose I was a derelict.
I was a derelict's kid. I succumbed
to man, and minotaurs were
a thing of the past – not
in my vocabulary. I knew the trees,
the fruit, the sweet, the fences
in my neighborhood to get me there
where dogs and men can't reach.
I beat the boys and joined
their clubs. No initiation
could deter me. Oh yeah.
I know where the tracks go,
how to catch it going South,
what to carry, who to talk to,
what size jar of instant coffee
will get you into camp –
how to walk like a child
of a maid: go inside the silk
hotels, wallpaper limned Inns,
at 10 a.m. the leftovers line
the galleys: ham and omelet,
waffle, cutlet, biscuit, gravy. . . .
I filled my skirt with jam and ate
through noon. I judged my troops
by the content of their refrigerator

(only ones with working moms
could pass). And oh, my literate
acquaintances! My bums and
babblers banging in the stacks!
I suppose I'm just like they are,
dry inside at last, pumping
the poems of Pushkin, Poe and
papers by the racks. I sat in there
most every day, 'whoring' working
hours away. I know the open places,
graves, the cemetery gate – only one
we're allowed to cross without eviction.
Idle tears will get you anywhere, said Tenny-
son. You can read it in our clothes, the rips
we care to camouflage or bunker in clunky
shoes and hand-me-nots, the stabs, the odds
of ever reaching our normality. I'd say I was
a derelict – I was a derelict's kid.

To David Without Goliath
From Penny Glass

David Nickleson, where would I be
without you? Nikodemus Greek,
as you liked to call yourself – skinny
16, squint-faced pole, face like an Okie
man – who would have imagined you
a philosopher, jug-eared and chicken-skinned
in a toga by the baths? You had a stack
of sci-fi fifty feet high & gave 'em all
to my brother – so spooked as you
were by a particular future. I spaced on
Monster mags, *Mad* and *Beyond*,
Tales of the Incredible,
while you and he bluesed-out,
dreaming of the playboys you would
someday be: He, *the greatest musician
since Chopin*, you, the *I don't know,
sumpthin.*

You were in love with an older woman,
*a blond, blue-eyed, 18 year old bombshell.
I don't know. She just likes me .*
You were the first
to say it: I was *pretty
smart, but not pretty.*

I called you from the phone booth
at The Spot, watched the men come
bumbling out the cantina and get
into their cars as we talked

for as long as the sun stayed
on the smoky horizon, 'til it got too black
to see. First, I told you I had heard you play
the coolest licks in the park. So I called you
just to say I thought you were real good.
That was the year I learned
gullible. *Sure,* you said,
I'm gullible to flattery
and a pretty face.

I wouldn't tell you who I was,
just described myself:
thin   16   5 - 5   long hair
red   brown   green   eyes.
I knew you couldn't keep a beat
and I was always a secret liar,
told the truth in a thousand disguises.
I knew all about music, talked bridges,
charts and chops, knew the bands,
the Russians, Nietzsche, *The Republic,*
and all that those Existentialists
were just coming on to.
I quoted poetry and Van Gogh,
turned you on to your first peyote mitote
and I was *a thousand miles away,*
stepping on glass in a pissed-up phone booth,
faking a girl from Willow Glen: *My mother*
has a "pool" and a divorce from my father
who's really "rich." Sure, we're paying
the rent, but that's only temporary.
She and I'll raise horses
just as soon as I find the right place.

I asked you if you read.
All my life, you said,

but I gave it up for cars.
I'd checked out all your books,
Fahrenheit 451, 1984, On the Beach.
There wasn't one I hadn't read
in that fifty feet of fantasy. Next
time I called you I had read everything
there was under "autos" in the stacks.
I called you just to ask you
if you knew how to fix my GTO
because I was really *a mechanic*
who's just having this problem
getting started.

You were impressed.
I could talk to you for years.
You said. We talked all of 1968.
I talked you through the butch
and a brutal father. You talked
me past my mother's divorce and her hidden
bottles. Time was suspended as much as me
that rainbowed year, and there it was: guns
in the ghetto, the revolution just
around the corner. And there I was –
stuck in a stinking phone booth pretending
to be me with another face and a steady allowance.
And there you were with your theories: *Big*
corporations are building underground caverns,
secret havens for cosmonauts to hide in
while they collect all this money for space
when everyone knows it
is mathematically impossible to resist
gravity. And when that first footage
came in you swore it was all *just fake.*
Just think of the bucks, you said,
hundreds of billions over time.

And when war broke out on that same screen
as the Ivory blonds selling buxom Cheer
you captured all the statistics, body counts
and names banking on an international
hoax of war. *Maybe it's just makeup.*
Hitler and Disney! Those guys can do anything .
They can pay to make millionaires of those guys
who pretend to die. They'll have enough money.

We talked the ins and outs of power, politics,
allegiances of billionaire people who were nothing
but black shifting Inc. on paper. You kept me
in the library when the *theoretical concept*
of suicide failed. And when you finally quit
your *Marilyn: her clothes and the fights*
and the bitch because she's really a closet
insomniac who watches too much TV,
didn't like your hippie friends and who
stayed up all night just to think of things
to tell you like why you insisted on resisting
the draft and hiding in your *"marijuana nutshell"*
when it was really me
you were in love with
from that very first call.

And when it finally came to that:
34-24-36
is what I cross-fingered
lied, knowing to you
that was *kind of skinny.*
You and her were *for sex,*
you said, *but honor is*
honor.

I did it for honor,
told you who I really was
after that summer of love
when flowers and peace were more profitable
through beautiful lies, and angels
were just coming into being in this life.
I told you then I wasn't no white girl,
but Steve's sister, the flattest sack
in the barrio you despised more
than you hated the rich.

No bunny in this booth

was all I said and it hung in the air
like the moths, horseflies and turkeydragons
smashed on the shattered pane.
That's ok. You can call me
tomorrow. I never called
and my phone never rang with you
on the other end. But it would never
have worked. You never could hold
your head to save your face.
I heard you got fat, joined
the Air Force, cut your hair –
but I dreamed
you were on that barrio bus,
same hair like a string of gold
water, same face
pocked like the moon
you swore
they'd never get to.

I just called you to say you taught me
the power of love,
you were the best I never had.

Cream

I'm so glad. I'm so glad.
I'm glad. I'm glad. I'm glad.

Glad to be young in the vat,
proud in a hat, splayed out
on the mat of the future.
"I'm so glad . . ." – but far
away boys were dying, splat
on the fat face of farce
and the market of foreign
frenzy. It was all about rice
or flowers. Opium and the sweet
meat of free sex. *I'm so glad.*
I'm so glad. I'm glad. I'm glad.
I'm glad. But it was all about
balling in the ballroom. Love
and anarchy keeping the
wind from your hair – NOT.
It was glad not to be hungry
but fasting. Glad to be fast,
to not be left behind,
scribbled from history
in a quest for meat,
the beast before
the cream.

Time Stands Still

Grandma had hands so strong
she could shuck an ear
in two swift moods,
leaving me, the silk,
for sweaty palms to strip.

The new kernels gleaming
like so many newborn butts,
ripe to the mistake and
spurting sperm. Grandma's hands
hesitating in the air when

she caught me – like swallow wings
at dusk when time stood
in the petrified wood
at the end of her garden
ache.

The White World of the Blind

It fell like flour shaken from my
grandmother's wood-grained hands,
the color of masa, a world
before the flame singed engraved
images on the flattened tortillas.
Dust dry coins, the petals of silence,
the only snow I knew before this bending
of the boughs and cracking at the seams
of the sycamores. All day, all dark,
it sprinkled its light, rearranged forms,
equalized. I saw through my window
the cold burning glow of the other side
of the globe: the white world of the blind.

Who Honestly Cares About the Next American Idol Winner?

She was searching
for the key of F.
Funk fables furring
her head, the perfect
make-up fading under red.
She was trying to make it,
hit the big, beat 'em up down
instead of getting beat up.
Her mother in the corner
throwing the first blows,
fixing the wrist she
shatters into slivers,
drips to a heart of lip
service: *Fat*. She was striving
for a dream that was already
broken, off the cuff,
in the rough, and off the key
of Freedom.

On the Poet Coming of Age

for Jim Harrison

there was this poet
    with Sartre's wandering eye
     he was cool
I was a street kid
   a moving sheet   of ice
    a floe   a cipher
 no moon
    the street lamps aired a golding
sulfur
gilded my skin
and the satin skirt
       I was naked under
swept   mooned   shells
   of light through the glassed asphalt

  seventeenandnobody'sgirl
       96 pounds of bad
burning
the midnight barrio   oil   lit
    a ticking flint
  he sat at the Five Star bar
       reading
Rupert Brooke   or Lowell how
     little now I

                    remember

                              just   the smoked pool
of light how he   (not the half-blind
                    poet, but the other   almostman)
sat squinting at the leaves of verse   I recall

                                                    how he

                    cradled the stump
                    in the pouch
                    of his denim
                    but

                    not his name
or the face   just
a beauty   the blank
boldness   and the   back lit
                            bustless

                                            pages
                    I never replaced   or
ever

                                        recaptured
        how I leaned on

                            the bar stool
        radiating   and   irradiating
            the sullen

                                                    drunks
                                        the demeaning mouths
a field
a force
there

                            parroting   passages
        of Neruda   Rimbaud   Baudelaire

a youth   remembering
youth
how hard   I owned whatever I said
whatever I touched
in those years
he was another
hemisphere   a continent   divided   by a man
made canal no side could claim
the jolt
that woke   his flesh   was not   the fire
bird
hand-painted   on satin
nor the
wild   flight of hair
but the English
I spoke   the enunciated
unexpected
he was
a poet from the Midwest,
he'd come to read Brooke   or Lowell
at the U
which I knew
was a lie
Cool
I said
and made a date for the Greyhound
knowing he'd go cruising for a better
lay
but when money   for beauty
failed

                    to pay
I took him and his wall-eyed friend   back to the old Victorian

there are these ships   see   you can   sail   without
course   an expanse of ocean   crossed
on a dare   choice   isn't limited
                        to Sartre
                        & Simone
                                    it's a game
the poor play
the wit's end

                            it was a game
out   guessing   out   reciting
out   smarting   the   legitimate
                    and the boy
I took to bed
                                    was sexed
when he undressed   my defeated
    city   he took   what could have been a fist
            from his pocket   the stump
        glowing milk in the smoking light
                            his gnawed-off paw
when I touched it he was soft thin

                                    a woman in a man
                            a girl
could love
he put it out   of sight

98

>   *If thine hand offend thee . . .*
>   *If thine heart deny thee . . .*   and with
>   a tenderness
>   for   an absence   I both
>   felt   and did not   I made   him
>   rise

>   swell   cliff
>   sail

fucking poets
>   he breathed   in the candled dark
>   as I tunneled
>   in all ways
>   that can be
>   taken
>   whispered
>   multi   pieced
>   lean as pricked goose meat

In the morning
the poet left by cab.
I walked him to the bus,
barefoot through the glass
and winoed streets. The other
left a poem about Mexicans,
depots, and the sullen poor.
All gone. I read it
and researched my 17
hungered years in the mirror,
and I dare it to say it:

>   *I am a poet.*

Art Books

Up from Canal Street, Bowery bound,
embedded glass chinks in my soles,
an old death's stickiness prevents my kick; passed
out, passed on, and pissed up men
color on the summer's vintage vine.

A real drunk's no danger, my sole
mantra. The liquid smoke of the festered men
marries the wind of the taxis, and passes
me up for a better fare, to the bound
feet of five-spice ducks, the smoked vine

of poignant sausage, the twisted guts of the man-
made drunks and the rank perfume in my soles,
kicked up, as they ooze and ache on Vine.
And I, a poet in New York without a pass:
caminando like the world's my barrio and not a bind.

I wrap my poverty shroud as I pass,
a refuge in my moonscape face, my sole
escape, an air of grace, my vine
grown hair wound about my neck. What man
can see me here? A young girl's binding

body sliding through her destiny – bound
for food stamps and the fiscal ides of passing
months: a welfare check by mail, my royalty, my sole
identification; named as nameless as the wordless men
who froth and clump and break apart without their vines.

(But I, I had a destiny, I was bound
for Art Books, a destination I had almost passed
in a telephone book from the booth on Vine.
I wanted all the words I couldn't buy, white sole,
maybe a vintage wine – this was my NY, yeah man!

And I was gettin' there with a street name, paseando
through the pissed-off nuts, the raving men
with my mother's breath: Fellows of the Vine –
same mauve displays below the brain, and bound
up rage knitting the face of fate without a soul.)

But there – Art Books! When I arrive: sole
displays without a trace of story, bindings
of neon or a mirrored text, a rambling vine
of readers through a blackened room, passing
cut-ups or one copied face – a repetition of men.

I am streaming past what I recognize, the sole
disgrace, my birthright written in a passing
text: the hand upon the child, a tether that binds
the family tie, a familiar bent of the derelict vine.
A real drunk's no danger, if he's with men,

but a mother passes the binding, vines
the letters with a branded hand, rips the pages solely
memorized, and fears the ending without a man.

Tierra y Libertad

pa' Cruz

That was another age. I held
you in my arms, drunkenly.
Your trembling moon gone
down the smogged horizon.
Your stunted form, your
survivor's heart, your steel
string thumbs working, painting
history in what little space we
wrested – stolen walls of pock-
marked chalk, matted colors
in a welfare jar. We partied on
the rented rooftops, in a hillside
slum on a rico street of glass
and Spanish tile. *One day,*
you said, *this will all be ours.*
And I believed. Our lives, a mural,
whatever booze-fogged doubts
blew in the autumnal ice
as, below, an automatic city
was acting, lit, ticking like
a turned off taxi emptied of its fare;
shut out, off limits, but entered
with flare, with our mind's machetes,
with opened books, with researched
words that kill and take back, with
impoverished looks.
                    I loved you
then; hated how you were dying

drop by dripping sip, your lips
drooling lyrics, rock-a-bye
binges in the eternal spring
of a young girl's drunken dualing eyes
rippling the floozy, madeup dawn.
The next sun's ours, you whispered.
And I believed. Now, twenty years
into that turning, a revolution done,
kantum sung, what little hope
we had is not ours yet. Your colibrí
Kachina dancer stalls at the edge
of a backroad wreck. Her wing pod
flurry hung by the heavy racke-
teering of Coors cans falling a Pepsi
Generation ago. O
                         Huitzilopotchli!
    Sysyphus
           Sisters!
                  Malled
mothers smeared black and red (roads
the hard hands know), if love
is not the answer, hate is not
the question. Warrior brothers, red-
eyed fathers, bruise-fisted, gifted sons
of bitches: rage and spurt
                        and memorize.
Forget the scent of Cuervo on a teenage
breast, the burning draw of rubber
on the outsider's chest; and I confess:
I don't believe. But do
            REFLECT.

"The Journey is Over"

for Ramon Del Castillo
upon being awarded his Ph.D.
15 de Mayo, 1999

says the voice on the phone.
"Doctor Del Castillo here.
I'm done, Lady, at last."

And I think of the mask of paint
on "King Crack," the black hood
of the past just over his left shoulder,

the calavera printing its sheaf of poems
in white and black over the faces
of our barrio youth, the jagged fingers

of Death stroking a ruca's cheek, boney
as a typewriter key striking out her future
as it shreds up all the unsigned diplomas.

But Doctor Del, Doctor Dell can spell.
He can fit it in the margins, analyze conquest
to a "T" for Terror, trading in tragedy

for the cape of academic avenger – and
DPS will never be the same. ¡Ajúa! And
the Denver cops will never take such easy aim

again. ¡Ajúa! And the next election better
count, 'cause Doctor Del can, and the data
is sorted and filed and compiled, and it doesn't

look grand for the master class. ¡Ajúa!
And Xicanismo is alive and well in
Doctor Del, rising like the muddied Colorado –

usurping the banks, resisting the shafted
concrete levees bent on holding us back,
rising out from the bloodied and battleworn

borders to irrigate the pock-marked fields
and isolated valles de familias, de víctimas.
Y los ancianos y niños, los indocumentados

y cruzados, los homies y homebound survivors
know: Este hombre no es vendido. They can
count on Doctor Del. They can call on

Doctor Del to spell. And now the stealers
of Colorado better do their homework. ¡Ajúa!
For today the revolution is a matter of degree.

"Is there a doctor in the house?" No, ese.
But sí, ya hay uno del Castillo: the King
is back, and he's got the crack, the wit, the plaque;

his placazo now "Piled higher and Deeper,"
this "Pinto highly Developed" como dice el otro
poeta del Chuco, Ricardo Sánchez de Aztlan.

Ya hay el rey, Del Castillo, con su pluma
en su mano y su six pack of libros soaking
en su mente. And to this Poeta highly Determined

con su Ph.D. y su "¿y qué?" I just wanted to say:
No, ese. The *battle* is finally over and won.
But the journey, carnal, the journey has just begun.

Collages: Una Despedida to the Summer Youth Leadership Institute

for El Centro de la Raza, 8/12/99

I. Karen

Karen's head is a heart,
her **Sueños de Realidad** hold it up high.
Her heart is an altar to the Virgin
y **BEBE** is the biggest word she knows.
"Tijuana" is close to the gut
along with **Jalisco" y "Mariachi**
but she stands on the power of poetry
y la musica de las mujeres holding brass.
With her **Latina** identity always on the right
I know esta torrera chiquitita, esta charra
de su pais, llena de dulce y verduras,
will forever slay the bull.

II. Marta

Marta con los ojos de oscuridad,
La Gata tiene mente de la Zapatista,
it overhangs hunger in a bare room
where a desperate family waits for an empty
pot to fill. El pecho is a smog-strewn
ciudad, but her heart has wings
to rise above it. Esta niña acariciendo
conejitos beside a sea of graves,
this woman of codices and pirámides
de los ancianos, con su ombligo de Tenochtitlan,
puts a premature baby in the palm of her hand
and walks over her inundacion
con la gracia de los delfines.

III. Ema

Ema con su pelo larga de las flores
y hojas frescas del arbol, do you know
you chose the golden ginkgo to adorn you,
tiara tree of memory and mind?
Pisces, with the heart of Mexico,
con la mapa de nuestra tierra engraved
upon you soul, the core of you
is calendario – for someday you will
birth your days, even when your silence
speaks the loudest, when your head
asks your heart, "Are you sharing too
much information about your business?"
There are fertile lilies and the red
flowers of potential inside you. There is
the fierce osa you keep tamed down
and a brilliant aguila waiting to arise.

IV. Vinh

Vinh, your head is an anglo map
pasted over the one you've drawn.
Vinh with the heart of Da Vinci,

whose car holds fast to the changing
freeway, with a world of flight paths
heavy on your shoulder, you long to play
with the carefree monkeys in the trees but
for the raging gorge of hunger. You hunger
for the jeweled lobster of the feast.
You travel on big ships, but there's
the little dog who looks behind him, at where
he's been. Vinh, traveling as fast as the dream
bike you glide on, but rooted
and determined as a garden that feeds,
you walk surely into your future, feathered
with sonrisas like an Asian
Phoenix, reborn.

V. Danny

Danny, with the empty head
and the branded dogs at the crotch.
Little fox with the killed rat in its mouth
and the lobos, tigres and a bronze lion
in the chest, there's a chained wolf-dog
at your core, a vulture on your side
that calls out a lean coyote for the fight.
Con tequila and the black sedan inside you,
I see the milpas and a rich river valley too,
a deserted beach in a tierra, unfounded.
Danny, a peregrine over your left
shoulder, the side of your death, flies
over the stranded dog on a sheet of ice.
With your good car dreams firmly in your fist
and the beautiful landscapes of your work

I know you will fill that empty living
room at the core with whatever you
imagine, whatever you want
you will.

VI. Cecilia

Cecilia, there is no **inside/OUT**
as you tell us, and **Hope** is
ALL YOU NEED. "The Hawaiian"
floats outside you on the other side
of "Heaven your brokedown palace."
Beautiful little Cc of the cut-out flowers
zipping across your knees, under
your purple heart of **Diego**, the heart
that **unlocks the forgiven places,**
there is the unclaimed village
of our ancestors, the untamed horses
that you will someday ride. You are all
telling, all words, except for the shoes,
those blue ones I see on your feet,
those real ones as you crouch
and leap, and someday make
real words escape.

VII. Sandra

Azteca warrior, La Reina de la
We Shall Overcome, Sandra, your heart
is half-filled with words about England

and half a patch of grass. Sandra
with the jaguar mask, with **the freedom**
of a butterfly. Mariposa primavera
at your core is Xipe Toltec, weaving
the skins of sacrificial virgins
into texts and the **memory of our land**
into fact. Slung upon your right hip
like a toddler is Chalchiuhtlicue, goddess
of water, provider of earth, salt y maíz.
With your right step firmly planted
on books, and centered as you are
on the demos y manifestaciónes de nuestra
libertad that grounds us, you will
stride into your life of **Help the
Community** and inscribe the codices
of history. Grrrrl, I know, someday
you're going to get that Lincoln Navigator
and drive your Chrysler Concorde home;
someday, girl, you gonna be
riding high in style.

VIII. Daniel

Daniel, my last blank page,
your unfilled collage hangs by the neck
with the upright others. Daniel, poised in the sign
of a little **G** thug, the blue outline
in a half-fetal crouch looks like a chalk
mark of death on the street. What will happen
to you, Daniel, the one that can spell?
"Travieso with an ESS," you correct me.
Ese, qué tal? You wouldn't come at all.

When you did you tore up every word
you wrote. You tore a hole through
the page – but with brilliance – some number,
some date, some coda for the cage
of La Jura. Locura, what got your goat? La Chiva?
At your core is the war, the history of the race,
La Raza de la Alma, El Calendário, placed
at the center of your will. You will – if
it's for your carnalas y carnales. You wrote
one for Ema que quisiéra

> *"ser un pajaro*
emplumado para/ volar sobre mares y rios/
y asi mirar a toda/ tu raza
que vive en tu/ México querido
eres como/ el sol Azteca porque tienes/
una meta de viajar/ por muchas tierras
y esto/ fue para la homie Ema."

You come when they call you.
Las homies called you on that final day
when your absence tore a hole
in the Sacred Hoop. You came late
but you would not write. I put it in

your hand, made you take it.
"This isn't a poem,"
I said. "This is your life." "Qué quieres hacer?"
"What do you *want*?" "Qué quieres?"
And you took the pen, and wrote
"Yo quiero the life of a sparkling star."
And tied it to a blue balloon. And with the others,
it rose, and overcame the broken hills of Seattle
like a dream, like an aguila finds its way
back to Aztlan.

IX. Emilio

Emilio, you won't stop writing.
187 in your head around the 4 directions
of booze, el cielo nublado de sus sueños,
and the running men along a barbed-wire
border and the beautiful rucas running
free. You won't stop writing. Your first
poem you ever wrote "the whole of"
in your fist, you won't let go of
the notebook. Con su patria querida
en su alma, and a stomach stacked
with unread books, and the office
chair you will never be invited to sit in,
Emilio, you won't stop writing
through your break. On the bottom
of your homie stance are the words,
"sending e-mail to the Boss from 'Home'
about being sick," and you won't
stop writing. Rap in your ear, you
swallow the big torta of your life;
with your barrio heart on the good side
y el Diablo on the other, you write
Emilio, you won't
stop it
you won't stop
writing

X.

todos tan juntos tan lindos
don't stop it
never stop writing
your life.

Poet's Progress

for Sandra Cisneros

I haven't been
much of anywhere –
books, my only voyage,
crossed no body
of water, seen nothing
other than trees change,
birds take shape – like a rare
Bee Hummingbird that once
hovered over the promise of salsa
in my garden: a feather-furred
vision from Cuba in Boulder,
a wetback, stowaway, refugee,
farther from home than me.

Now, snow spatters its foreign
starch across the lawn gone
crisp in freeze. I know
nothing tropical survives
long in this season. I pull
the last leeks from the frozen
earth, smell their slender tubular
tubercular lives, stand
in the sleet whiteout
of December: roots
draw in, threads of relatives
expand while solitude, the core,
that slick-headed fist of self, is
cool as my dog's nose and pungent
with resistance.

Now when
the red-bellied woodpecker
calls his response to a California
owl; now, when the wound
transformer in the womb
slackens; and I wait
for potential: all
the lives I have
yet to name,
all my life
I have willed into being
alive and brittle
with the icy
past.

And it's enough now,
listening, counting the unknown
arachnids and hormigas
who share my love of less
sweeping.
For this is what I wanted, come to,
left alone
with anything but
those girlhood horrors –
the touching, the hungry
leaden meltdown of the hours,
or the future: round
negation, black
suction of the heart's
conception. *Save me*
from a stupid life! I prayed.
Leave me anything but
a stupid life.

And that's poetry.

PLAY

PLAY

Play three: Journal of A Cuckold's Year

A Note on *Play*

Play owes its being to Natalie Goldberg for a variation of her exercise in *Writing Down the Bones*. We write down the first thing we think of: a writing topic, a word, a phrase ("first thought, best thought"), and place it in a hat. We pull out a slip of paper and I time-keep: seven minutes. Then, we each read our poem aloud, either in a circle or "Quaker Meeting Style" – as the Spirit moves us – but all have to read what is written. We go in rounds of four or five. No comments. Just hearing the variations. Soon, the imagery and music interweave. Some of these poems are made up of twenty or so quotations, "shaggy" or "buttery" words written on the blackboard. A few are made up of random words taken from various poems (as the titles indicate). Some are scattered throughout *The First Quartet*. "Find them!"

I call these my 7 Minute Poems. All are unrevised except for punctuation. All are spontaneous, with given titles. They are centered spokes on the wheel, as they remain.

– LDC

How Little You Know the Poor

How little you know the poor.
Wrenched away in your enclave of hypnopompic
cleanliness, the vagrant heart doesn't
stand a chance at the button past servitude
on a dime. Dímele the idea of a dive
of saliva, the worm of ramification issuing
out your pores at the prog of a policeman's baton. Here,
in America, in the US of AA, you, at the hoist of a hoax.

Forgiveness Like a One-Winged Dove

scrambles in the sand. At her peace,
the Pacific rubbing at the ruts and gouged
out eyes of shell; at her feet, torn feathers
drifting in the sea breeze like the dollar
bills he crumpled and threw at her leaving.
On her face, two ripe plums the size
of the ones she picked at ten. One
has split its skin; she wishes she were
a butterfly coming into being, and not this
lumpy moth, too many and muddy to be
admired or collected. "Forgive me," he recites,
and she washes her feet in the brine.
"Forgive me," he repeats, and his
stuck record sticks in her craw as he strikes
out.

Pure Sunlight, Unfiltered, Unviolated

penetrated the lacy curtains,
insinuating across the mussed
up bed and warming her thighs
like a hand. She had just
showered for the sixth time
that day and she held out
her hand to the offering, the
reminder, the possibility
of something else – another
way of loving.

Not Here

"Not here," she says, and diverts
the stream. "Not here," she whispers
and converts the lunar waves. "Not
here," she sings and prevents
the clots of summer from settling
on her skin. "Not here," she murmurs,
and currents desire into tidepools.
"Not here," she startles in the thicket
and looks away. "Not here," she confronts
my gaze like a deer in the bristling meadow,
and returns to feed.

Copper Kettle

In our splintered house copper
was a gift from the gods, found
pennies tail side up, the sparking
wires of used appliances, the inside
layer of the quarters we were never
allowed pressed to silver like the missing
meat in our sandwiches. Now,
I find myself, heads up in Leadville,
mocking marmots on the bald divide,
the rocking earth of glinting ore
beneath my feet: pennied, receiving
and singing for my supper.

Baby Doll Dress

How I hated those pasty faces,
that drag of fray on the cuffs,
that cracked tear of the chipped glass,
staring, that fake blue of the sea.
All my dolls were naked, stripped
of their mute and crippled artiface.
And the grey cats were gleaming
in their lace and buttoned collars,
in their bonny bonnets & braided silk trimmings.
What elegant teas we had, hunger
our only mistress of manners,
seated like Mad Hatters, my tuna-
tamed tigers and I.

I Lead the Night in Their Shadows

and follow the killing floor where leaves
let go like suicidal children and
let flow all around like dancing figures
in the final act. To say it isn't true
but not say it. To pray it isn't true
but not pay it; the coffin man with
the silver lining, the obituaries copy.
I open the door and look out to sea
and think of expanses of an element
with the taste for tears.

Manzanita

whorls in a clingy abrazo, witchy
arms around me, forearms hard
and mahoganied as grandma's lifting
water; what survives fire, survives
conquest, digs down with stubborn
tendrils. How I loved you, "no sissy"
tree, naturalized native, your
hair enthralled the crows and rabbits
nuzzled their spines against your burnished trunk.
When the last acorn is leached from
the land, you will aspire.

The Golden Pears of the Christ Child's Mother

Peritas de San Juan is what
they called you, Grandma, slender
saddled mare. Your silver spurs
you left behind, you let it lead you
through the bouldered paths, the
lichen-licked cliffs. You married late,
too wild-haired for golden things.
Freedom of the setting sun, romance
of the rain. Men were cane,
staffs for the threshing. Lashed
tongues tried to sway you.
Heavy breasted. Peritas de
San Juan. You kept them to you
like the golden pears of the Christ
Child's mother.

Childhood

The man in the booth is talking
about Spirit and the physical
body, how the "plasticine of
childhood" is molded into "Self."
How the body is shaped through
the spiritual forces manifest
through the environment. My son
is making balls from his tortilla.
Taco, taco, he says as he feeds
them to his muñeco. *Cookie.*
Cookie. Boom, agua. The woman
in the booth hardly gets a word in:
Experience. Uh huh. Experience . . .
she murmurs as the man drones on
about pushing through the layers
of enlightenment. *Boom, agua.*
Beach, my baby says,
remembering Yemáya who almost
reclaimed him, how the Pacific
swelled over his 18-month old body
as he watches the rain now dissolve
the day outside the window.
Boom, agua.

Childhood, II

Snail slime on the swords
of jello, lime green cool
to the touch. A Navy pillar,
a coat with brass buttons.
Waiting. The amber fill

of glass. The pass of whiskey

in the park. The promise
of splash, a pool of presence

in the naked bulb of light;

someone stroking my hair.

I am poor. I don't know why.

"Good Writing Makes Me Cry,"

my mother said, crying
into her beer. The beer,
the color of a cross in piss;
the beer, the color of a stained
page; the beer, slurring old love
into tears; the beer, foaming
up the glass like a rabid rat.

"Good writing makes me cry,"
she said, listening to some failed actress
read Elizabeth B. Browning into
dawn. "How do I love you?/ Let me
count the..." days, I thought, the
sleepless nights, the hours of
stolen dreams. How many times
can you hear one stupid poem?
A song? How many times, "The Shadow
of your Smile" like "Who's on
first?" or "Slowly I turn, step
by step...?" A bad joke. Until it grabs you,
until it yanks you off your feet,
all the wasted hours and wasted
words: a Remembrance of Things Past.

The Garage Light, Foggy and Dust-licked

holds the smell of a lost kitten, retrieved
months later as a bramble of fluff
and twig. The light diffuses into
the ash of her death, a mother
beaten into submission, into gray dust,
into the memory of an orphaned daughter.
Everything happens in absence, the last
leaf turns to the page of dirt, milk
curdles into old love, an outgrown tennis shoe
left on the walk. Remnants of acts
and inaction, now riddling the shafts
of sun with their dance, and the burnt
aroma of packaged loss.

She Was Holding Impossible Dreams
Like They Were a Collection of Sea Shells

Their sharp edges of folded
hands hurt her heart. She fingered
the sandy ridges of their embrace,
smooth inner flesh formed
by sandstorms and flood. Her tears,
dry now, flaking the tender skin
below her eyes – all of her,
opening, ungrasping, undone.
The sunrise sheen of her,
brightening, lightening, becoming
possible, becoming.

Monkey

I never saw the caged monkey
at La Borda. He shivered and sweat
behind the rusted wire by the hotel pool.
His silver ruff, his matted paws,
his claws, long from under-use, his
lemur eyes tearing from the mine dust –
all this I imagine. Scrawny is how
my companions described him. Silent as silk,
padding in circles or staring, simply
gazing at the sheened swimmers.
What was his crime that he came to be
reborn in this solitary cell in the
aged hacienda of a silver baron?
Will some traveler, one day, open . . .

The Heart in a Cage

He troubled my sleep, crooning
a la roo roo niño with another.
Phantom lover, divorced other,
why return between the roosters' challenge?
I dream him: husband of fifteen years past,
in a stone cavern, a cage of jade.
I am snipping branches of bougainvillea,
not too quickly or I'd bleed and purple
climbing roses the color of clots.
Something I must do, prune away
the aged to make way for a sweeter
scent: engorged blossoms the heft
of a heart. He attempts to evict me,
says, "It's enough now. How much
can you cut?" But does he think
I want to stay, listening to him singing
the song of my sleeping child
with her, the better voice?

Frank Sonata by Candlelight

She listens to Frank Sonata by candlelight,
wipes her fingertips after a dip
of lemon and rose, cracks
her crab with a silver plier. She
never bounces a check, always
remembers to buckle her seat belt,
never skips breakfast or forgets
the way you like your toast
and coffee. Light and creamy.
Have you forgotten Satie
moving about the house like
an elephant trunk, a melancholy
plunking like autumn leaves or
wood smoke in the morning? How
they found him, alone, wasted, dis-
heveled in the head and reeking.
No one paid the light bill
that year. I listen in the dark.

Migration

Called to the window before first light.
First married one, you, dreaming into my pillow.
A movement of trumpets, a percussion
of wings, and I see them, stitching
the sycamores to stratus. First geese,
large as basters on the west coast
by the bay, soaring out of story books,
the pages I thought were lies, happily
ever afters, hundreds in a drunken vee.
I think of them now, married
in my mind to the dream of wild parrots,
the untutored talking to the sky.
The flocks no one believes exist.
The long lost tribes, revived.

Opening

They're opening the next scenic
way into your chest hair, 17
mile drive down to your hairpin
curve where the breakwater stuns
and the sea lions beg and the pearls
are like petrified frog eggs.
Twisted cypress, tormented
waves and your miracle mile's
sleek as new pave.

Hope

Too small for foreign coins,
Too rare for an antique store,
Too wide to fit the furious child,
Too sweet to meet the gaze.

A light goes on in the quarry,
A glint shoots off the bay,
A shade falls on the glaciered pass,
A sword of shadow lifts from the heart.

All marriage vows fasten like stays,
All tapestries pass the needle's test,
All mercury dances an accurate pace,
All this that waits, all that which doesn't hate.

Old Shoes

You were like old shoes
I can't throw away, a record
player still spinning, my
coffee maker with the holes
plugged up. I wish I could
drain you, sing you, walk
you 'round the moon. My baby
got no cash, no class, no cracks
up the seams and shining grease,
flapping and slapping my sole,
you let in the breeze,
ride me just right, stuck
in the groove of another era:
sweet, but obsolete.

Jambalaya

When I hear that fiddle tune
I see her overgrown gown
and black-booted shoe, Latoya
sings her favorite song. And she,
the other woman, the apex of our
fete, keeps time with a squeaking
bow. She was never any good.
That hurt the worst. That no talent
bum, good only for cutting oysters –
smelling of boiled shrimp
as you cut the rug across our license,
cut the ring off your hand with a silver string,
Latoya sang: "Me and Joe, we
gotta go, me o my o."

Say What You Mean

but mean what you say,
and live it like you say it,
mean it like you love it.

Grandma knew – every conejito
has her hole, every pajarito
trills his note, every marrancito

chews his bone. And you?
Private as a whale, silent
as a worm, homey as a dirty rug.

Say what you mean. Say what?
You can't mean that. Say it isn't so.
Say, why'd ya have to be so mean?

Thelonious Monk

Play a circle around the note,
said Mingus, but there was three
of him: one here, one there, the
other off to nowhere. Porkpie Hat,
The Prez, a shadow with a sax.
Man said, *Play it like you hear it,*
say it like you mean it, live it
like you'll die it. Monk shade,
a hair lip time, Monk sun,
a rising cane, a willow stalk,
yellow liver, smoke whisper
in curly hair. Ivory and coal
wood, knuckle and shale, nail
tinkling, moaning, slowing
'round the note, *'Round Midnight.*

Crying Trumpets

When Stachmo sang the blues
he knew better than the punk
kid that he was, smokin' that reefer
on Beale Street – he kept his mouth
shut. Satchel Mouth. Satchmo',
counting on those pennies from heaven
that didn't come from the white man's hand.
He wrenched that satchel wide and
filled it with pride, that empty sack
with a black boy's stride, filling his living
with music. And when he hit the big
time, big screen, his silver dollar days,
they dressed him like a monkee in a porter's
suit, a bell hop's braid, and Billie
played the maid. They both sang
crying trumpets.

Blackbird

Working the field to hay, the hand
knows the corner of the callous. Over
the sweated sun, avenues of rays
divide the harvest into seasons. One
fine seed becomes a horsebale, one
rare sheath becomes a reddening bleed.
Lashed to the wind, the winding rolls
of paper, a slaved day becomes a
fugitive army. The blackbird steals
the way.

Tattoo Nation

A girl is lost
after getting off the bus.
On a destination through the southwest,
a girl is lost.
Getting off her transport:
a plastic watch, a yellow
cloth bag, a walkman. . . .
"She took a walk, man,"
and disappeared into the heat.
Her companions in the blue
hair, in the green mohawk,
in the chains of a round
trip ticket. A car waits
in the parking lot. Her relatives
have no Kleenex. Her skin
may be parchment or meat,
may be pierced, may be scribbled.
Her tattoos, now, her Nation.
Her jangling name, an anthem.

Indigenous

Earth, the color of a scab.
Indigenous eyes, the hardness
of shale. Indigenous sky,
colorless. Wind wakes
the wanting of the weeds.
Fire frees the founding of the fence.
The sea slays the slicing
of the seasons. Rock
rocks the rocking of rage
into stone. Let it turn you
to salt. Let it lick you into
rapids. Make it see you
into stars. Wish it will
you into flight. The old
moon is just the flairing of rage.
The listening lapping is just.

Dancing

Tomatillos bending on the vine,
maravillas tossing manes,
rios and the smiles they carry
on their waves, water spiders,
dragonflies line the banks
like rucas of the band.

Give me your hand. Dáme tu
cariño. Ritmo wind and maraca
rain. You were put here
to place the step on Mother Earth,
to turn. All that shakes controls
the seasons. All that moves is
dancing death.

Tiny Shadows of Leaves

You were born on a patch of dirt
named for a grid of uncharted
desert. Your grandparents fled
The Long March and disappeared
into blood canyons rather than stand
disappeared and bloodied. Your mother
never washed a dish in her life, but pressed
the spines of cut cactus together
which dried into bowls. Your sutures
never healed when you lost them both.
Your father's heart, too small. Your
mother's heart, too large. You scraped
the arroyos of roots and hard seeds,
mouthed a language too clumsy for
your tongue and tried to forge
love from the tiny shadows of leaves
in a foreign country – your own.

Multiplication

Four plus zero is a corner in New York
where Lucky plays a pinball sax for change.
One plus one can change your life.
Two times two can grow a family
out of home. Three times six
is a crowded classroom in Jersey
where Maria doesn't have her homework and
Aaron swears too many times one.
Five times five is a banquet on the Upper
East Side where six time six many pigeons
are poisoned into the slams of traffic.
Seven times seven is the number of junkies
nodding. Eight minus seven is the
rhythm of the wait.

Shut Eyes

There were no pennies
for your eyes, no cross
to bear, no ex to stir
shut the stare. Your face,
an empty vase, the trace
of you there, in the shadow
of your oozing breath,
the flatline silence
in a winsome wait.
Your last request
takes up residence
in the air, a silver vapor
like sparkler trails
finds home in the white azalea.

Overcome

Overcome, she stalled
like a '54 Chevie, put her
hands on the wheel and turned
them, star-faced, palm up.
She has only these hands
to feed from an empty refrigerator,
only her squeezed-shut eyes
to cut off the engine of her
hunger, only a mouth full
of petals and perfume, only
her silence and her braking
at the corner, at the edge.

Searching for a Thought

I picked a plum instead.
I rubbed the sweet skin,
smelled the blood inside,
opened it for the first and last.
Its breath was still warm
from the sun's abrazo, rivers
of tart sinews flowed through
the veins. I heard the ghosts
of birds in its seed, saw
the flesh shine with tiny mirrors,
and tasted the firm ripe body
of my mind.

PLAY
THREE

Journal of
A Cuckold's Year

Disruption in the World is Green

The gray sap rising.
The willow writhing.
The forest ripening.
The fern frond frightening.
The furred ant is unfurling.

Disruption in the world is
a green dress on a dream date,
the final pricks of daffodils
usurping the riven earth,
the fine beard of rye in the furrows,
the frenzy of confetti
and the green face of a St. Patrick's wake.

1/23/03

Yo-Yos and Peanut Butter

You go up and down
the misery bush,
flashing sparks of yourself
sloughed up the line,
the strings you hang on,
all Mother May and If I
Might and tiptoe through
the two lips of some lost
relation. Relations (bumpy
as the chink and slide, the info
ride) decide to paste it
up. Brilliant. Do you die?
Do you run out of thread,
do you threaten up the replay.
Repay, the joking lie.
Eat up the slack. Alack;
and return.

1/23/03

Juice

He got juiced up tuesday,
jived up the marmot bag
who barred his way to graduation,
got jammed up on a jam note,
forgot the 'ho', was pining
to load up. Stuck up on Sally
riding on a wave of jizz/jes
yesterday, road up on a wave
of sanity, got juiced up,
fueled up, mumbled all the way
to saturday.

1/23/03

You Make Me Wonder What the Rest of Your Poetry is Like

If all the words lie flat
like the knap of a cat's back,
do you ruffle up the grain
and arch your hacking cough?
Do you rabble up the rouse
or scrabble down the brain?
I will refrain from fame
blast, repasts, reposts
or get backs.

1/23/03

She Hated Men in Discount Underwear

And she hated men in silk.
She hated men in fresh top
running shoes, and she hated men
in weather. She hated men
in perfect polyester and
she hated men from last semester.
She hated men in flannel shirts
and she hated men who were late
for work. She hated men
in pimpy record stores and she
hated men in raves. She hated
men on ocean cruises, and she
hated men in waves.

1/23/03

Axe Heads Hanging Off the Tops
of Capitalized Letters,
Like the Letter "T" for Example

got in the way. They were
always in the way, telling their
tails, waving their broken he-arts,
coming down hard, following through.
Axe-heads, hanging off the tops
of fallen trees, the great
get back, the fine and weighty
bread, the crumbs of loss and
losing it to a "T".
Axe-heads, ask heads, marvel
at the lot. Revel in marble
heads that fell off, resigned
to kudos telling all, and fired.

1/23/03

Bananas and Peanut Butter

She suspects he's a banana
& peanut butter kind of guy,
corn-raised and hell-bred
retread from the factory
of failed marriages &
brokered dreams. A queen's
share of glitter would get her
way. A regular wage by way
of So. Hampton. Her mardi
gras to spring, a silver beaded sin,
a flat knife dine, a steady spread, and
not to tear the bread.

9/2/03

Just a Postcard from My Dreams

You arrived, "just a postcard
from your dreams," you said, like a jackalope,
a hybrid lover, long-necked
long-legged patched-up trouble.
A new kind of vision
for the Arizona sun, the
Texans flatlands fingering
up the onion of your tears.
A new kind of hombre, no way
passing. Through.

9/2/03

Sultry

September was a sultry
egg. Hairline cracks
beneath the skin,

the window of unseeable
moss that did us in.
The bats flared up

from the navel of river,
they conjured up the musty
sunset, a sprawl

of risen wing, a feathering
of vanishing summer, an odor
of loss, of new leather,

of ten pennies in a soggy
pocket. You looked up
and a ripple-limned love

crossed your eye.

9/2/03

Faded Embrace

He had skin like a gecko,
little faded boy, the flush
of rage, a pink page
on each cheek, a weighted
cage just under his breath.
He held his head, inhaled
his dread, his mother
squeezing the pulp of him
down to zero and juice.
It was a faded embrace.
A great escape, she took him on,
the bruise of her grasp,
a cluster of grapes.

9/2/03

With a Thickness

You arranged yourself
with a thickness, dank padded
shell, wellness, a word
of the past, you cast
yourself aside, inside,
the riven passage, a
whole redux, the useless
passion. Then everything
was apricot. was a way
to yodel down the loss.
All the missing, all the
uninflated. You made it
an art, a way of walking,
a walk of wonder; and the slab.

9/4/03

Thundering Beat of Hummingbird Wings

All around us: migration,
the great pull of catharsis,
the rising of the daffodil
and out, to the sea of disaster,

the crisp purple leaf, the
final dust, a crimping
curl of drought. No doubt,
a rummaging hush to menacing

cold, the sudden season, the thundering
beat of hummingbird wings.

9/4/03

Infarction

It was just a hard sell
from the factory, just a cellular
tic, just a missed trick
of the body watch,
just God cashing in her chips,
just a nick off the old clock,
just a stop and a holding the line,
just a toeing to cow towing,
just a hospital bed, just
a corner on the market; dead.

9/4/03

Jelly Doughnuts on Your Breath

and a KitKat in your desk,
Almond Mounds adding to your nalgas
and ice cream in the fridge.
It wasn't me who made you fat.

It was all that. And the racket
of sell on the telly, the ratchet
of wellness pulling the pawl,
the hatchet of habit going to work.

And the town, the town, the courage
of managerial drink, an unclean sink,
a lay-off and a stink, and you,
who were never a bit of all that.

9/4/03

Hat

Showed up showered up, shoved up
shiny shoes, showed up
as what I shouldn't use,
showed up like a line of blues.

You were just what I needed
yesterday, or last before that,
or that year when all the borders
vanished, and showed up on my floor.

You were there, like the Cat
in the Hat, grinning your Cheshire
cattle guard, giving up the last
wee notes and letters like a

secret weapon, like an unarticulated
desire, and the last spot to clean is you.

9/4/03

Obtuse

He was too obtuse to live,
or, is that, stupid? Too stooped
to live upright, too uptight
to give full light to the will.

He wouldn't answer you directly,
pulled a moment out of his hat
and called it a Cat-o-Nines. Tried
to sell the flavor of lies in a

vocabulary packet. Fished all the fries
out of a sack and savored the salt.
Sent a regiment of syllables
up the river to do their time

and no one has yet to find
the definition of the ruse.

9/4/03

Benevolence

He had the benevolence
of a cat, declawed,
pissed off. He was tame
when all the fur fell
in a knap, when his hair
was unruffled. He opened
the door to the refrigerator
of his soul, sounded
the alarm set off in his
throat. You couldn't touch him,
wouldn't stay in the heart
long enough to rule any
kingdom wider than a pocket.

1/27/04

Lazy Raccoon

he said, and meant her,
the hazy-headed blonde
in the too-tight button shirt.
But those hands
are anything but, they see
it all, furrow it out
of the muck, wash it all, dry.
"Lazy Raccoon," he said
and her mascara had run
a marathon of lunar nights
til lonely was a song
out of hell. All those banded
together lines, all that
masking when they colored
the kitchen. She took
out the garbage. He ate
all the nuts.

1/27/04

Childhood III

Childhood, for him, was like one
of those faceless figures
in a Tony Ortega painting.
Mr. Everyman: vibrant,
in living color and a dead
mask. He put on his childhood
like a pair of old boots –
only when the threat of rain
became a desire. Memories,
like photos, came to the album
of his senses, to be matched
to the outfit of soul, a scuffed
shoe, a broken buckle, the missing
left.

1/29/04

Untitled II

You were all alone, a juiced robot
in a puddle of drone,
tempered, gyrating
in a slither of salt, soothed
and lathered with sex, enthralled
in a lexicon of wait and a condescending
smile, enamored with the buzz of lonely
linoleum underfoot, a look that smote
the dust, a torque of an undone heart,
an inebriated caterpillar of sweat
taming the brow, aluminum azaleas
in your eyes, a modified swallow
licking the monkey rhymes
off your tongue down to the singular
knickers.

9/16/03

Perplexed

As if
I could ignore
the innocence of the ocean,
that crisp drip of equivocation
in her zealous flesh,
the thrust of her sugar reverberating
in sun-spray, the dewy abyss
of that sanctuary of fresh
in the heaving peanut butter waves
that paralyzes with obtuse
angles, the angels of oasis singing
down the sun to the color of an open
ham sandwich eating up the dusk.

9/18/03

Ghosts

Something sparking overhead –
the dead? Someone hard of hearing,
the heaving breath, the left.

Who's calling up the ghosts?
Calling down the heart.
Calling out the ghosts
of art, the many unawares.

12/3/03

Letters to David

An Elegiac Mass
in the Form of a Train

for David A. Kennedy
1955 – 1984

If all time is eternally present
All time is redeemable.
But what might have been is an abstraction
Remaining a perpetual possibility
Only in a world of speculation.
What might have been and what has been
Point to one end, which is always present.

– T. S. Eliot

from "Burnt Norton"

Letters to David

Note to David

from Journal Entry – April 25, 1984

Today, goddamned David Kennedy drank himself to death. After holing up in a Palm Beach hotel suite he was found on the floor of his room between two king-sized waterbeds.

Two beds! It rang through my ears like a mantra. Two beds. $250 a day he paid for that room & most of the time he stayed in the downstairs bar. Cops couldn't find evidence of any hard drugs, only the vodkas and grapefruit juice the bellhops said he drank steadily from 8 in the morning until 12 at night every day.

I picked the paper off the kitchen table which is mostly littered with my books from the night before: Prescott's *Conquest of Mexico & Conquest of Peru*, *The Fall* by Albert Camus, an aesthetics anthology, *Portrait of the Artist As A Young Dog* by the Welsh poet, Dylan Thomas, *A Handbook of Style*, The MLA Guidelines for submitting papers, Nathaniel West's *Day of the Locust*, Marcuse's *One Dimensional Man.* I start reading the accompanying articles about the trials & tribulations of life as a Kennedy as I pick up my, by now, lukewarm coffee and head back to the room, over-stepping the fish-hooked shards of glass from a broken lightbulb.

"When he was only 12 years old, young David stayed up in his hotel room late at night and watched his father on television. A family friend found him seated in front of the set switching the channels to the different news broadcasts to watch the tape play over and over. The friend recalled that there were no tears, only a look of stunned horror."

"The day before, on a family outing, the senator had saved David's life when the boy was being swept away in an undertow."

I remember the day Robert Kennedy was assassinated. I remember it better than when the President was shot. I felt it more. I was in the seventh grade, and that was the first year I was ever truly aware of politics or the wars of the world. That was the day the next door neighbor poisoned my pet cat to keep it off her lawn. I remember the sweet smell, like bitter almonds some say, but to me it smelled like she was was vomiting rock candy. When I found her I could tell by the way she looked at me that it was too late to save her. I didn't even bother to call anyone. Just held her stiff, wretching body & I remember I didn't cry. I felt solid, smooth, like ice but dry, warm. I remember the sun that June morning. It burned the hairs on my arms & I remember how strange the heat felt, like needles of radiation entering in through the pores in my skin. It was numbing me. I held her on the ground. She was too convulsive to hold in my arms and I tried to tell her that. The ants around us were swarming as if excited by the smell of her cooling flesh. I stopped watching her die and smashed ants. Sick. They were so many frantic kamikazis. I wondered if it was a sin. So much minute life snuffed out could leave a blotch on my soul like murder.

I put the paper down and go to the desk by the window. Under it is a cardboard box where I keep a lot of old stuff. In case there's ever a fire, I plan to heave it out & then jump out after it. I don't even have to look for the diary. I know exactly where it is. I reach in between the notebooks and pull it out. I turn the leaves to the page as I lie back in my bed. *June 2, 1968. Today, Robert Kennedy was shot! Kitty died.*

That was the day I learned the word: *apocalyptic.*

– L.D. Cervantes

First Station

(June 5, 1968)

I remember
it was a very
hard day
there were
buds
the size
of plums
on the
sugar tree
daddy
was a word
wandering
in the night
your daddy
talked
nationwide
the chosen
prince
you were on
the doorstep
of his shoes
between two
worlds
in that LA
motel
you were in
your pajamas
he was on

the floor
I remember
the sun
was very hot
you were in
a worldwide
Disneyland
your dad
the TV mascot
through the race
wars I spent
my life
ducking
the bullets
from
duck!
I said
duck!
bombs
came
through the
worn hole
of my elegant
dreaming
only crackpots
dream
in color
only the insane
order flowers
the color
of living
blood you
ordered
your life

ended
ripped
from the script
that day
the red
anemone
burst
your eyes
glued
to the set
your eyes
still holding
that vast
expression
rapt as
St. Francis
Receiving the
Stigmata
that morning
they found you
stuck between
two beds
in your Brazilian
Court suite
you hung
a painted flower
over your head
your last
request
still for art
they call you
an artist
they call you
the other

victim
in an endless
film loop
the willful
repeater
in your dreams
you heard
the shot
over and over
again
saw
the bloom
swell
saw it drop
I duck
in the dream
American satellites
killers
every one
falling
indiscriminately
from the sky
armed junk heaps
US stars and stripes
forever
painted
on the side
like a piece
of Jasper's
Rauschenberg's
falling
the way
the sky looked
dripping

not rainbows
but anemones
beautiful
watercolors
I remember
white phosphorous
burning through
the debris
of five months
before your
superman
pulled you
from the tow
the life was
saved
but the knife
left a hole
the size
of a needle
mark
on my skin
and the red
flower
bloomed
on my pants
brown
as the blood
of a father
gone
fifteen years
dead
the flower
you said
was very sexy

you were seduced
she was very
sorry
for your father
as the plum
was ready
to split
she turned on
the set
duck !
I said
duck !
but the
television
showed it all
cowboys and
gangsters
young girls
stalked
young boys
getting ripped
from the horse

Second Station

(June 4, 1968)

there was
something
to say
that day
he said it
all with that
first sleek
look
that smile
not made
for the gaze
that look
the cameras
never caged
the hero's
tape rolled
just for you
that line
he cracks
when the mike
shuts off
crooned
just
for you
that essential
cue
that punch line
missed
by the mass

there was
something
you needed
to say
having heard
there
in the surf
what you
needed said
again and again
like the rippling
of heavy breathing
not heard
but seen
with the grace
of Baryshnikov
as he lifted
you from
the riptide
furrows
that sucked
you in
its opening
flower
Don't die
he said
We don't want
any losers
in this camp
and how
the joke
transforms
the hook
the burr

of the fix
see
how the twisted
weeds affect
the sea
you go in
and it's all
hands down
he said it
all
with lights
and action
and a photo
on the front
page
in the moment
after
that timed
persistence
you and he
solid
as dolphins
skimming the
dimpled dumps
of water
back to the
waving
wharf of
flashbulbs
the break tide
marshland
cracking up
like school
girls giggling

in Neptune's
maniacal
webbing
and there was
no way
to explain it
and it broke
you up
everything
cracked up
and the mesh
never mended

Third Station

(Fall, 1974)

we were
the same age
in a decade
of curious
parallels
or parallel-o-
grams of folded
cut-out
paper
what they don't
understand
is that
it's not
the shot
it's the subtler
juxtapositions
that drive you
insane
or to the
drug
that shuts it
off
what they don't
understand
is the world
gone
Laugh-In
when every
image

strikes
home
a divine
metaphor
you hear
the family
name
you hear
yourself
the brunt of
an irresistible
joke
I think of you
Easter
folding
the coke
into neat
parallelograms
"Sno-Seals"
for your snorting
friends
did you think
of your uncle's
"Christmas seals"
did you know
they would
call you
generous
for this
did you think
of the family
penchant
for practical
jokes

of Ethyl
still driving
the family
car
BOBBY
is the last
you ever see
when she
goes

Fourth Station

you are gone
but you find
your
self
in a book
a major
chapter
in a gothic
tragedy
you have
a hand in
while I
could expect
no invitation
to the writing
of my history
you were
a page
unrolling
a life
unraveling
in their nightly
Teletype
machines
your every
error
a national
event
the year
you went
to Harvard

I met you
on the stairway
going up
you were
going down
they said
that fall
you are
a walking
death
in the interview
for the school
paper
you
are slamming
your fist
on the studio
desk
I'm mad
you said
I'm just
mad at the
whole fucking
world
what you never
understood
what you
were just
finding out
was the thing
he tried
to tell you
what he never
had the time

to tell
the family
is a walking
gallery
ducks
on the track
that summer
you are a
rich kid
I go with
my mother
every month
to pick up
the check
to some
it is only
a job
to others
it is the
cross
they elect
to bear

Fifth Station

(Fall, 1979)

that morning
they find you
I am still up
from the fix
my connection
and I
had gone
on
in the night
about money
desire
and work
money
is obsolete
I go
work
is what
we desire
wage
is an illusion
physics
makes everything
physical
poetry
we don't need
the symbol
anymore
you're insane
he says

and he fixes
my car
for pay
he asks
what I do
that is
so honest
I tell him
I write
stories
to make
my living
and sense
from the world
he laughs
his knowing
laugh
he asks
what book
ever changed
the world?
I go
Bible
and Marx
wrote a book
that's grounds
for the war
you're going
to die in
he laughs
again
passes
my lines
I go

I know why
we are fighting
why the ones
who have
your face
have the power
and the others
who look
like me
are the poor
statistics
I finger
the powder
I go
here
is your living
I hold up
the hundred
here
is their
death
we stare
into the other
eye
he has
seen it
honest
to god
he has
been there
before
and knows
how many bodies
there are

Sixth Station

(November 6, 1982)

I do not
profess
to under
stand you
I remember
when Tragedy
was only
a hit tune
I thought
I would
never croon
baby again
I remember
that night
before calling
from St. Louis
the star
of Walker
Art Center
in Minneapolis
I was telling
my stories
they
were asking
what is it
like
to live
in the bay-rio?

aren't you
afraid?
I remember
them milkfed
I remember
them
straight teeth
I remember
my sophistication
and the flight
back home
to the nightly
news
to *the bloodiest*
weekend
in the city's
history
I remember
my mother's
face
on the screen
my city's
most brutal
case
our house
gone up
black
in his flame
and I watched it
glistening
another
livid tale
of the battered
and burnt

lifestyles
of the poor
before
some kind
of light
switches me
back
to general
electric
general motors
general Bechtel
general ITT
and general
dynamic's
allied engineering
I shut it
off
I think
of you
on the floor
of that sleazy
Harlem hotel
the *shooting*
gallery
tv said
shoot up
to shut up
cowboy
but beware
the black
men in black
they might have
something
black
to tell you

Seventh Station

(Fall, 1982)

Kennedy
democrat
ethnic
Catholic
family
like mine
I think
I know
you
best
how they
shot you
at a party
and you
were a real
asshole
in that photo
from Xenon's
you are holding
your two
impossible
dates
the twinned
extensions
of your dual
nature
one strangles
the white
model

she's stressed
but still pretty
while the real
actress in line
the native
woman
your family
denies
is more beautiful
yet you
and her
are distant
distant
as the
distant wreck
that left
a heart
maimed
a love left
lifeless
left estranged
left crippled
left rusted
in the summer
of '71
something new
settled in
your vision
left you
estranged
a snowfield
a snow blind
paralysis
sets in

like a father
you hold it
steady
by clenching
your fist
and your host
in the other

Eighth Station

(April 25, 1984)

the morning
you die
I go
watch
trains
die
in the tunnel
near my
burnt
house
there is a place
where the over
pass peaks
and the smell
fills
the air
the creek
the canneries
with the stench
of burnt
papas
in oil
same smell
in the fifteen
years
since
I came
to this track

to die
to dive
into that tunnel
or rather
to watch
the progression
of cars
my blood
still rumbles
shooting
a hole
from
the heart
in a loop
to the mind
to the folded
up packet
I still have
in my jeans
Jesus
was a sailor
when he walked
upon the water
was what
I'd croon
as the cars
headlong
in front of me
smashed
assassination
through the tunnel
with the music
of acid rock

and the cars
behind me
swooshed
and honked
seduction
seduction
seduction
hummed
in that
image
I'd see
on the track
the instantaneous
smash
is what
we all love
from that
act
I'd imagine
the crack
like a shot
as I hit
from that
distance
it's a question
of practice
a need
to get it
just
right
by imagining
a bass line
backbeat

mainline
rhythm track
that keeps
us on
the back
of that bridge
like a spent
buck
what you
and I
together
understand
is that
they don't
know shit
when they
say
you did it
to forget
you never
forget
you always
remember
you talk
and something
listens
the sentient
being
that basks
in the know
nothing
soul
the soul's
mate

Ninth Station

(April 26, 1984)

I go
in the house
there is a
back door
I have
the key to
it opens
on a joke
I go
what smells
like burning?
I go
O
and laugh
synchronicity
cry
simultaneity
I think
of you
joining
the joke
and we go
get beer
I buy two
for I have
your company
I sit in
her room

I open
the bottle
offer
the other
to you
my old room
left strangely
in tack
dirty bed
curtains
the smoked
Motherwell's
flanking
the walls
like *Elegies*
for the Spanish
Republic
I wish
we could talk
about abstract
expressionism
about you
and Bobby
hitch-hiking
to elect
poverty
for president
did you ever
come out
my way
did you ever
confess
or did you
know

they
would tell
of you
crying
in your pillow
was that
the price
and demand
for the telling
for the silence
for the life
of the victim
who pays
it smells
like hell
in here
he'll tell you
that's
what will
cost you
he'll tell you
my insurance
man
ranges
a description
of the damage
there are sealers
and scrapers
but they
cost you
better
knock it
down

better
start over
what happened
here anyway
you would know
why
it is easy
to hate
why comedy
is the purer
form
I take it
out
for you
lay it
on the line
here
is our mirror
not gold
not metal
but gilt
some kind
of plaster
and paint
knock it
off
remember
that line
from the sixties
about color
compatibilities
twinned auras
particular
particles

ions and
hadrons
quantum
quarks
when we die
inaugurating
love
in the heavens
with our
blesséd
names
for at least
three days
in a row
where are you
now
I imagine
you here
where do you
go
to the most
familiar
do you go
where they
need you
to the most
of them
wanting you
needing
your name
in their black
books
in their
filings

everything
they want
I have
and they
can't
understand
why I don't
use it
to the fullest
you said
you would
never

use it
you could
never
be the president
you would
never
be a millionaire
you could
never
judge the law
you would
never
join the military
that was out
of the question
you would
not be
a clerk
a priest
a lawyer
a martyr

you did not
love
school
you would not
write
the novel
you could not
fault
your father
you could not
find
the truth
in the papers
with every ink
spot of rust
on the needle
you would
never be
alone
you would
always be
surrounded
by silencers
the silver
bullet
in every
crank

Tenth Station

(April 27, 1984)

heroin
is to horse
what cocaine
is to saddle
what snow
is to muteness
what brown
is to shadow
what monkey
is
to what
monkey
sees
and says
the talk
that shuts
up
grief
shuts up
the criminals
turns us into
sharp shots
like vodka
like grapefruit
is
to a drunk

what they
never discuss
is the gun
how the bullet
could enter
here
and come out
there
do you
remember
that hole
the questions
unanswered
and them
telling you
logic
is reason
enough
to phrase
the question
correctly
is purpose
enough
not the justice
of the answer
but a show
of finesse
in the asking
did you slam
your fist
at that one

Eleventh Station

(1984)

shoot
is what
they
always
say
the polite
for pain
the junkie
for pleasure
the gambler
for god
the lover
for prayer
the friend
for talk
the killer
for life
the creep
when he comes
into you
back off
is what
they always
say
shoot
is what
they say
when they mean
back off

Twelfth Station

(Lent, 1985)

don't touch
this house
it's worth
a mint
in deductions
you
and I
could laugh
we could pat
each other's
back
clear
the other's
throat
we could toast
and coke
and beam up
to that man
who tells us
there is nothing
intrinsic
separating
the class
from the
masses
I go back
to the connection
there was
this debt

I had meant
to pay
it came
in a dream
of the mind
freed
from its
body
debt
hey
I go
the reason
I'm late
is I've been
writing
a story
about David
It's about
time
he says
out of
the blue
and I know
he knows
I mean
you
he knows
I mean
to use you
as they use
us
whenever
they put us
under

that blue
ruled light
we still have
the shadows
to play
for ourselves
we are
the guns
the ducks
on the screen
it's our finger
on the trigger
on the button
on the dial
on the switch
that shuts
it off
don't touch
these walls
it's not
your mess
don't clean
up after them
the dirt
won't wash
you'll need
ammonia
alcohol
ether
the works
the men
who ruined
your father
are the jail

and the jailers
and the key
let them
spell it out
in plain terms
in the language
and logic
they teach us
to lock us
into eloquent
and profitable
lies
don't touch
this house
these walls
this negative
relief map
of the bombed
out
forces
fine
as baby
soot
it exudes
and stains
and it won't
come clean
it's all
that's left
of the ashen
cross
on your
forehead
something

Thirteenth Station

(Easter, 1986)

Did you do it
for your father
David
did Goliath
go down
to the nth
degree
in a sea
of hero
ism
what else
could you do
we do
what we
have to
your father's
father
made a mint
for the family
liquor industry
did you
toast up
to them
to a brand
name
beaming on
your tv screen
did you toast
to the Russians

did you toast
in gest-
ure of
camaraderie
what a trickster
you joker
it was Easter
on the Florida
coastline
same light
same sky
same sucked heat
same etiquette
of denial
same stuck
up smiles
same
buck up
face
little soldier
same poor
misguided
missiles
they launched
through the eyes
same tow
haired tyke
set adrift
on the tide
same season
I know
there are
reunions
the heart

can't bear
to go to
I feel it
myself
in the wind
of an Indian
summer
when leaves
let go
like suicidal
children
and everywhere
I go
I remember
and forget
that she's dead
where's daddy?
you were asking
that weekend
that island
odyssey
they sent
you on
American
Family
Robinson
you
fresh picked
from the surf
saved kid
still rubbing
your eyes
from the salt
where's daddy?

and why
were the questions
shut up
in your head
why
where's mommy?
and they were
only too
quick
to tell me

Fourteenth Station

(June 5, 1986)

your father
was on
the tv
my mother
was in
the bar
she was
drinking vodka
he was
drinking vodka
he followed
her home
she was
a sitting
duck
I know
your father
was almost
the president
my mother
was a drunk
but we all
cry
in our hearts
when death
is too strong
there were
mistakes
on both sides

said the judge
your father
was guilty
said the conspiracists
my mother
was guilty
says the conspiracy
of her court
boy
I see you
as you were
then
a fine blue
the color
of sky
when seen
through a hole
shot through
the fog
by the direct
laser
will
of God
I throw it away
he gives me
some extra
do it
for David
he goes
I do

Hard Drive

Love is itself unmoving,
Only the cause and end of movement,
Timeless, and undesiring
Except in the aspect of time
Caught in the form of limitation
Between un-being and being. . . .

Ridiculous the waste sad time
Stretching before and after.

– T. S. Eliot

Porta Lee is a few hundred yards from home when she sees her grand-daughters, Cilla and Sandra, sneaking across the irrigation ditch. She doesn't call to them, and off they go again, hoping and twirling into the fields. She pulls the truck up onto the lot directly in front of the house and sits there beside Mr. Will. Sweet, warm air blows in through the windows across them, and there are dandelions and wild asters she hadn't noticed before coming up all around. She wants to be pleased, astonished; winter's gone, but what the doctor in Forrest City said about Mr. Will's heart has left her "just so tired." She knows she needs to get her husband into the house, bathe him, and put him to bed, but all she can do is stare at her hands, at the criss-crossing lines, the callouses, the raised, lead-colored scars. If it was night time, she would be looking up into the sky for answers.

– Eugene Richards

Hard Drive

Striking Ash

On Line

Con una poca de gracia

Striking Ash

(to be salvaged)

1980-81, 1984-89

Love in New York

Snow sifted in strands
upon the slicked elms.
It settled in the branches,
gentle as my fan of black
would be upon your chest; the waft
at the thought of your hair
made me ache from the cold
of wanting you – your love, the sick
sparrow of your heart. You understand.
This love, the nest it's found. My better
dreams, my inner day, are all inextricable
in you, my woven secret. My breath
in a sigh is angel's hair on a sub-zero
morning, murmmuring your name; you,
holding up the winds that could take me
away sure as the brief word no.

It'll never be.
This train I'm on runs south.
I'm pure as a certain wall
of sadness, nothing muddled
in this sleep of loss or never had.
If I could be with you here
there'd be sun, blinding beauty
binding to a sheet of ice. It cuts
straight to a light so sheer, a set of gold
fingers currying your hair – I adore you.

Though my hands are bundled
deep in the throat – this heart,
this secret icing – a winter plum.

Driving Home From An All Night

for Steve

We skinned the night
like hawks cupping the air
for the best we could get
wherever it would take us.
It was an all-night. And in the after
hours you talked, I talked, your hands
dribbling rhythms over the table, the mirror,
the glass; speaking spells & voodoo
mojos about dreams and the power
of leaving – how we never get.
"Why can't we just mate like wolves?"
I said. "Is it ever just simple?"
You asked. "Sure," I said. Simple.
But I couldn't tell you how.
Each word kept canceling the other
so that none of it got said.
So what could I say?
In this life we're either rising
or residue. That is the choice.
We watch the world tilt,
the sun raise her grinning mons
above the balding root of freeway –
there's a coupled radiance; the head
lights sucked to the source
of the oncoming traffic – such simple
ghosts dancing to raise a diminished tribe.

Go home, I said.
The day is rising.
And what can we do?
Except get in the car
and drive.

Striking Ash

If I sleep at all
it is safe past the death's
head of wolves' hour
after the final chink
in the sky closes
when entire worlds shift
predawned and dusked
I dream
if I dream at all
when the utter
silence of you gone
gushes out
when the sentries
of the past ignite
these mute
birds into flutterings
of love

love is the standard key to open any lock

how is it that death
should become inconspicuous
how is it that death
is so inconspicuously
blunt
a bludgeon

a photo
a report
soot
some words

your hair
there
where there
was once
your light

'til a mean luck wrenched you from my hands

I walk a brief circle
around our house
slack before the spent
frame where we lived
listless as shells

as if no one else can hear or see in this bright house

as you mother
dreamed of somebody
you could be
frugal not fragile
taking the measure
of handed-down shoes
so when the slay
of the land
taught you to beg
and pray
you laid down
your arms
bit the quick
of nails
and began living
the intricate pass
of the blinding stitches
of those who labor
in waiting

in labor
for love of

'til a wicked luck refuses the link

your father's depression
house housed the
pawnshop you hated
the violin he forced you
to play you scraped the horse
strings up and down
the worked spine
cursing that old man
for never knowing
his girl's hands
could settle like birds
flocking
whitling ivory

nude islanders stirring surf and ebony from a wooden world

for never letting you
come down hard on the key
that would open your life
your Pandora's box
broken into from birth
you dreamed of knowing
Chopin and harmonizing
wind with a music so welding
it wedded with a lilt
worn with the utter loneliness

of that place you heard you could play

in the backroom where
your father never goes
where the beaten
marimba is stored
you used it clean
a wooden substitute
for humming out
the trapped voices
hammering out the battered
chords of thieved lands
your mother's gift
her hands answering
the questions Chopin
leaves you

love is the common bludgeon to jimmy any window

grief is never civil
it comes to your door
at the thieves hour
like a social worker
from the sixties
it comes crashing
in   to yards
of four roses
and checks
through the curtains
to see who's sleeping
in your bed
and do you
deserve
the benefits
of the poor

what could I have done with you shaming me past my senses?

you are gone
and still you are
dragging me with you
islanded here
sleepless child
helpless before the tow
past colored treats
past dolls' heads
past dripping wrecks
drunks or the kittens
purring in the bush
usher me anywhere
mother
I learn
why we come here
striking ash
off what we've loved

because love was what it was we put our trust in time

between seeming and seance
words and science
this is what lingers
snapped shut in the heart
and fated
all that infant
wanting
you waited all your life

as I now wait for you

time doesn't heal
it cuts the cord

we become ourselves
for a final fling
absent from the source
a fish in air
air in a globe
of tears

in a light that boils and burns

did we love our mothers enough
as the air
does the time ever come
when we hand our mothers
the china we are
and say *mira*

look what you have done with blood and air

did I love you enough
ask the page
this clipping of you
this brief and always gift

hustling grief past its prime

ask the air
this science
where I find
evidence of you
this soot
irrevocably spoken

From the Heights of Machu Picchu

While there I sat
perched upon my grandma's
swing fixed upon

The Heights of Machu Picchu,
sunset spiders crammed
their beaded curtains studded

with the jade of flinted, sparking
flies; the dance of spider
feet: pause, pleå, the bad

dream of running, going
nowhere, spinning paws like
dogs, like prey, silent,

webbed across the poles
of sway and swagger: my play,
protagonist and ploy

against the impeccable blue
of Califas winter. Women
the size of acorns ruled

those linear nests. Summers,
not so conspicuous, set
my sights on autumn and in

the drift of smoke, in my wooded
future I sniffed the air's mundane
authority. Not for me to heed

the action or ever need
a script to toll and tell
my all, my dead. Ticking

like a clock, I metronomed
my way through lines
that caught my hair

inside the gears of that machinery
of my lifted action, and pulled me,
head-first under the spell of my

imagination. Neruda and the swinging
patent leather segunda shoes
would sound the hours I sat.

My buzzing adolescent frame
stilled inside that web of flies,
fruit and buried towers. Flowers,

air to air, the floor-length curtain
of red and clotted blood, and
ivy snaked with twisting

arms and rat tails, crickets
and their running engines fenced
antennae, cast silhouettes of boxers

poised and winning – all
of this I watched, mastered,
with an other eye, listening;

quivering feelers inside
me as the poem
unfolds.

Sleeping Around
(On Dead Pablo's Birthday)

It seems I am tired
of being a woman. I walk
the gray plastic streets, my
umbrella in hand, unharmed,
brewing my serpents and ash.
I take apart glass, rear it up,
spend another day ironing
imaginary tigers to a base
of unpretentions. I filter the water,
the water like glass, the glass
fallen apart at the axle: *my*
ovaries can, my ovaries can,
like a stalled engine gasping
for a break. I break apart
bread that smells like my vulva, that
flashes me signals of desire, acres
of leavened wheat in the earth
colored blend of my muscular
thighs. Would I lie
to you? Soft-spoken and de-
lyred, a veil over my mouth
imagined, too, but an obstacle.

It seems I am tired
of playing at dying at the sink
of another ides of my livid month,
my body, a breakwater, there in the
foaming sex surf. Great elephants
of men chain and lumber through

a dream of running – my caked
feet upended in the game of mud,
not quite dirt, and not quite
crystal. I walk the waking
streets, awake and clicking
my heels at the great escape.
Were I not prey I would not
pray to the idols of Paris,
to the fine hairs of Helen.
I wear my shoes down
to the holes in the soles
of this cardboard city – all
the loaves halving and cleaving, all
the ovens bursting with ribbons
of children: the winsome ones,
the winnowed whiney – all captured
in the gas, in the living
will of Autumn chased by Summer:
chaste, but for age; chased,
but for an age.

It seems I am tired of putting on
shoes that hurt me, of a
sorrowing street, a dress
where I no longer live, the hide
of something once sleek
wrenched inside-out, a vagina;
but for beauty's sake – a long
division of snake in the rattle,
a hand bag of poppies, the bright
teeth of a girl. It seems I am tired
but the sleep of queens
grips the baseboards of
poverty, opens her skirt

there to the pulsing, presses
her finger in, frightening day
lilies flouncing in a florid orange,
bounding over the fences of a range
of possibility: the heaving, the shy
one, the forgotten bitch, the
aloe ally – all these
in a civilized stroll and beaten down
to taro root, a nurturing fog
that is not me. While he
exists.

1984

for Susan who liked the poem,
"Hope is a Thing With Feathers"

When first we, trembling,
read about the rats
aloud to each other
in your mother's
scrub-faced kitchen
there was no other
hand to hold
except our own
no other book
we could read
in the months
following
so profound a gospel
surrounded us
that soap operas
died in us that day
never again to trust
that cool blue
televised
surveillance
that came of age
in the '60s
of our 13th spring

but this is a man's world

but it wouldn't mean nothing
you would always explain

so what was left for us
to do but be
the toughest
boys on our block
there wasn't much
we feared those days
we'd feared a lot
and felt it less
we could take it
in a man's world
fake it
but like the girls
we were
we shuddered
at the rat's resolve
to devour us
so that afterwards
the mere gesture
of a wrinkling nose
or show of unbraced
teeth would set
our nerves on edge
worse
than the teacher's
misplaced chalk
or the fear of bombs

hope
to us then
was
a thing with feathers
it flushed up
around and passed us
hope left us
somewhere between

that windy day
the sexual revolution
blessed you
with a childhood
motherhood
and The Revolution
lefts us with
50,000 warheads
like maiden heads
in war waiting
maids in waiting
on this
the advent
of our 30th year
of prophecy

but this is a man's world

and Susan
it's a man's world still
there isn't much that's changed
except the fear
is more sophisticated
educated
into a fine composure
tomboys like us
now take on technology
click their heels
into reams of data

there's some for the stars
some for the riches
some for the sea
'$ of bitches
some for the oil

some for uranium
and all for profit

none for the amber fields of gain
none for a cheaper medicine
none for the seed to be left behind
our legacy
a final blossom
of undisposed
mushrooming
post-industry

this is a man's world Susan

we've more than rats to fear
hope is a thing with feathers
to a woman

but to some man
hope is a thing
with guns

Whole Lotto Love

I believed it was only a matter
of language, that two-headed
sword: apples y naranjas, a long
division, a blunt-kissed mouth.

I learned
about mud from the tide down,
about rain from the lightning up,
about roses from the taproot
shorn at the waist, about silk
and decay from the kernal in,
about seediness from the beaten
pulp out. But it's all
in how you say it/ ¿Cómo se dice?
Dígame/ Spell it out/ ¿Oye
cómo va?/ Au revoir/

Logos digs its own
grave free, the mirage
is in the numbers or prime
division – a stone hard cash-
ing in of the elements, quick
picks of thieving lust
where winner takes all
and the losers lose
off ten.

On Line

To Line on Our Forty-Somethingth Birthday

Things are not as they seem, nor are they otherwise.
  – Dogen

Everything is water if you look long enough.
  – Robert Creeley

Because the earth has dissolved into the memory
of our bracketing coasts and the black inquisitive soul
at the end of a seagull's beak probes past summer,
because yesterday morning rose from a wrinkled journal
like the crooked finger of smoke before the fan and your
hair turns another shade of ash one night at a time,
because the rain-soaked streets cast out their fat
threads of red worms like the bad taste in the mouth
after kissing another willing loser and shutting the door
one final time, because the sweet silly saliva spits out
when we talk past the wolf's hour, because we are
approaching that silence, when the crack between
worlds widens like the hips of a beautiful woman
and I dream of old lovers leaving through the portal
of the sea, because there are birds, because there is
this flame that keeps lighting your cigarette and
an old record still spins in my vulva when the rain
strums off the skin of an aging poet, because this time
the pages scatter like leaves on my floor and dragonflies
mate on wing, and everything lets go like the dandruff
of our days, because you will crumple your Times
differently today and we will note but not follow
the scope of our separate horrors, because regret
is never anything but and sorrow is an archaic term

best left to the diddlers and dawdlers that line
the bus stops and subways, because we have nowhere
to go this day, and our mother's special pain radiates
from the grave, because the season is preternatural
and no one but you knows what this means, because
maybe someone will stroke the dappled fur of your
belly, absently, like placating the kneading cat at
the crotch, because I will not, because all of my
clocks have stopped at varying times and I allow it,
because your watch gets less notice than the piano
riff of a dead jazz junkie, because you are not
a junkie, because I have this wood under silk,
because you have that ball of fluff under wood,
because our poetry is not as idiomorphic as the skin
of Hiroshima bomb victims, because we are survivors
and it's never not inane to say so, because you say it,
because you just note the weight of a stranger's breast
impassively like yesterday's game scores, because I
only imagine you do, because passion is denied
in name only, and the bastard child, our hearts,
stays nameless at the tip of a tongue, because maybe
there are tongues and you'd laugh at my insistence
upon that coming-of-age ritual I crave, because you crave
a certain saxophone of the flushed, because we are flush
with it, flushed from the grave like these old newsreels
of radiation damage that ruin our celebrations, because
we are celebrating, because the best party's under the gleaming
fingertip, because the echo of our names stays locked in the tunnel
at rush hour, because you no longer lean on the horn,
because I am no longer lean but I can still delight
at the approach of my weight equal to my IQ, because
I admit to you this vanity, because you are restless as
the silver-backed alpha pacing the den and your wolfen
eyes have never met mine, with our shadowed faces

sheened like the thoroughfares that keep me indoors
and writing this, because I will never be older
than your age, because I admit mine, because I admit,
I admit that the luster of turbines no longer holds
the thrall of space or cybernetic spittle through digits
of light and absence; because you are absent and my
fingers ache but are pretty, I admit the call of lint,
the crawling through scuffed shoes while searching
for the dime that knows your home number, because
you are ten numbers away from a voice, because mine
cuts across the memory-fields in a search-and-destroy
mission unique to my sex, because our lives of language
and time can never find the rhyme for fuck, I admit it;
I admit that the day is rusty and slack; I admit that
the age is something other than nude dancers on a stage
or the flailing air-guitars of the disengaged; I admit
that lonely is not a word that occurs to me often, but now,
in the rustling waves of stop and go traffic, I make out
your face from the passing, deforested, paves and I
wish you a day, innocuous and useful as pine or the blade;
I'm hoping you're getting it, and you smile; and I wish
you . . .

one more line.

Titillating

desires tittilant. Must be hardriven
to create. Procreation optional.
Maturation required. No vice
or versa. Verses or versions
of life-crimes can poetaste
elsewhere. Very nice and
categorically imperative. Kant-
ian walker without a watch or
Wordsworthian wanderer with an eye
for lit, longhaired ladies please dial 9
and then hang up.

Why I Don't Date White Men

He wouldn't walk me home late through the barrio
lamps, wouldn't rise to the challenge of my name,
would have affairs of the jugular kind in the
race wars of his mind. Remembrances of
seldom seen faces, revisions on the silver screen,
places of labials and the rolling of tongues, character-
istics as genetic as the taste for salt, races
of sunshine, exploring avenues of bombed-out places,
smoke from Tezcatlipoca's obsidian grace –
all this and more would gash a gape in memory's
gate; at the door, a messenger waits, the tickets
to the next opening of desire is at your nape. Do you dare?

Fate with a magical wing takes perch –
in the double take, the steady brake. I heard
it said that autumn is the cruelest fate. It
snows all night and midnight too.

For He Who Wants to Know

You want a poem for how my nipples
feel, raisins in your ear, sunstruck
in your rolling thumbs, hard little
clits wet with your suck. You want

a poem for summer breasts, for the wipe
of silk on your pelt. You want an orange
the heft of a grapefruit, the wedge of pulp
between my legs, the sweet flush of sage

burning for you, for our ancestors remembering
the jump of a woman shuddering in lightning grace
when the words rush out in a whoosh of the
pluck: like picking cotton bolls, like never

splitting the skin of the grape, like a man
in the hand the weight of a bird and beating
hummingbird hearts against my thigh. You want
in? I hold you out. I arrest you against my

nipples, rub you between my sacs of wine
thirsty for your taste. Teeth me like a man.
Scrub your chin brush into my neck as you pinch
and knead. Like the button that turns on the world.

Like the lamp that lumes to the touch. Like
relámpago. Like the stunned timber. Like
the falcon's eye to the twitch. Like the growing
mouse sliding through my sopping hands. Like

the tail. Like the tale that gets longer. Like
the telling dance on the tongue. Like the tip
of the ay! Like the globe of the moon waxing
from a cloud. Like a motorcycle's hot key

turning alive under your thumb. Like the leap
between your legs at the twist of a wrist. Like
your kiss. Like your kiss. Like your kiss. Like
my lips up the shaft. Like you. Y como nada más.

Son: Book I

The province of the world
rises. The poem, when it comes down,
is dark.
                    – from a fragment of "Paterson,"
                    William Carlos Williams

Reface:

rigor, beauty, quest.
"But how will you find beauty?"
When to make a start
out of rolling up the sum?
Defective dog among a lot
of dogs, rabbits, the lame
deceive assuredly – since we
know beyond our own. Yet,
rolling chaos, nine month wonder,
the city can't be otherwise. Rolling
drunk. Sober ignorance. A certain knowledge
and knowledge undoing. (The seed
packed sour, lost, off in the same
scum)

Rolling, rolling, heavy with
the ignorant sun, the slot of never
in this world save dying – dying,
yet that is the addition – walking,
subverted by writing. Stale. . .
Like beds made up, unable.

          Rolling, top
thrust and recoil, a great
wash of seas –
from divided to regathered
into a river:
       shell
       man
       to son.

I. Line of the Giant

Lies in the spent waters,
lies in the thunder of dreams!
Asleep, dreams walk the city,
persist. Incognito butterflies
settle on stone; immortal and seldom
the subtleties of his machinations,
the noise of river automatons who
because they know the sill of their
disappointments walk, bodies locked
in desires – Say it, no
things – nothing but the blank trees,
forked preconception, accident – stained
into body.

From higher than the oozy abandoned
beds, dead withered mud thick with dead –
the river comes. The city crashes – the edge
of recoil. And rainbow
language unravels, combed into a rock's
man, a woman like love. Innumerable.

                                                    But

only one city.

          poems   return   embarrass
          more woman than poet
          living
          an investigation   bolted forever
          hope   publicwelfare   do-good like

The waters – the brink, thought –
cut aside but forever strain,
strike-marked by a seeming to forget
later replaced – they coalesce now
quiet or at the close conclusion,
and fall, fall, split apart, drunk
with the catastrophe of the unsupported:
a thunder struck all lightness.
Lost; regained in the fury, driving
to rebound, coming – keeping
to the stream of connotative 'equal' –
coeval void.

And there, her head carved by the quiet:
Colored; the secret temperate him,
his Valley of the Rocks, asleep.

I Was Born; But Not Quite News

Lorna,
Lost Land of the Deer, loner
Who lives in words on moss dry rock, lichen quartzite quarry,
A lover of long vowels & longer sentences, stray milleniums
    of pleasure,
Who notices a sunset's fable, the inflection of oak, parched
    landscapes beyond the potted plant,
Who feels the thirst inside but goes out into the marsh feeling
    the blades of lost,
Who learns folly from the firefly, mumbling from the stoic
    moose,
Who dreams . . . . or hopes . . . . . or wishes . . . . . . Not!
Lorna Dee Cervantes,
A person who picks apart the paper – and is not anewsed.

Con una poca de gracia

Portrait of the Poet at 33

Your favorite photo's "Pain."
You can't describe it. "It's Life," you say.
I see the river swollen to torrent.
Behind me is the house where a grocer lived
scribbling his bits of poetry to big-breasted
girls. His life stacked up around him,
the layers like fossilized shale: old
obsessions, fey larks, snapshots of a siren
blond daughter and a sullen black teen
he calls his son – asking me to explain it
to him, as I understand "these things
of the skin." I see eyes that cried
for nineteen hours, the shark in my gut
recounting a rape; in my brain:
a full-blooded Choctaw, mad
with injustice and art, the silver-toothed
grooves of a record spinning the lax
loves of my life into graying hair.
See the lines in the photograph?
The past is a blur. Wind has furrowed
my brow with stray hairs. See that latent
forehead of the cornered grouse?
You see a portrait of the poet, determined
as the thigh-length salmon spawning in the west.
I see a girl in a Oaxacan shirt,
a two-headed chicken at her breast –
two cocks on either side of a divided
heart – her only savage choice.
I see the breadth of Pacific behind her,
and remnants of shells 5 million years sealed.

And look! Glossy-eyed cows in the distance,
a herd of seals breathless with foam.
I am aging past the photograph,
toward you, toward
all of the above.

First Beating

for Javi

What a strong little sucker you are!
All my grit and guts rolled up in a fist.
All I ever had was strength: head
strong, heart strong, even my genius,
tempered, impermeable; all my soggy wishes
hard-boiled away early, nothing but blades
of glass in the end, fused to the bottom
of my past, bitter crystals shimmering and
there for good.
               From these damaged goods,
I pass you the flame, my ware. Alive
in your sea of blood and spit and piss
your ventricles unfurl, hurl into space
like the hands of maíz, the thick pricks
of daffodils asserting through the wimpy dirt.
You beat a good goddamn through the conjugal
mush, up between the aged cracks in my skin,
through my pores I hear it rapping: first poem,
first flush of wings and separation. You give
me this: a heart like a jackhammer tearing
up my world. Oh my little secret weapon, self
made slayer, you are mine. My strength. Your own.

Now

You think you are
the Master of the World
because you now know
"plus." You know
"infinity plus infinity is
infinity." What a mass
of wire and pulse
you've become from a blast
of cells in my coraline
mush, a hush of uncertainty
inside me. All is stance
and bray, kick and spray,
now that this mass and
Master of Mess is "five
and six quarters." Lord
and Lawyer of the Universe,
pronounce me now, "Best Mami,"
here in your sleep, in your hero
dreaming where I root, that
shifting grammar, that infinite
arena where you count.

Homing

When first we arrived
you leapt como las toninas,
from air to sea to me.
It was here you were conceived,

this coral dirt you recognize
on sight or smell. You fell
into your element. Salt-licked
stranger, what star passed you,

touch of Venus from Ixchel?
We wove your bones together.
We droned dirges to the solitude,
sacrificed mollusks and crusts

of bread burned by hungry mothers.
While you twisted into art,
thread your way into my womb
strips of fluid passed

on. Fighter from Yemáya,
part woe, part weed, full seed.
Fire from your father's eyes, brimming
solar flames on the night you came.

Who could have predicted you?
What card foretold you, the Child
of Crystals retrieved from Nortes,
the trade wind's lust. I'll keep

your bracelet of sighs. I'll wear
your harp player's hands mutely
signing in the dark. Where do you
flee in your dreams? They come

to me como olas o el sonido
de mi corazón. Steady riser,
you pull me from my sleep,
tide-ridden, busted through

like a full moon clouded over.
I wish you – defeated by none.
I'll free you, wolfen one,
when the crack between worlds

opens, when ancestral spirits
stray, like you, to earth,
to birth, to land, to see
me.

Water Bearer

Lagartija bonita, did you bring
me messages from the rain?
Wearing your green linen suit,
your patches of denim, your
fly-colored eyes, a spy-catcher's
glance. With the hummingbird's
tongue you've come here by
my hand like a vision I've
remembered. I tell you I loved
him. Here, in your tumbled
down house, we first made love,
first kissed, first matted skin
and bred. Before my poet's
eyes caught fire from his coal,
before his purple hands brushed
my breasts like paint, you were
hidden in the stony coral,
listening with the wind. You
sang it then: the song
of moving tides, the clinging,
passing; underfoot and barely
seen, seeding freedom
in the slide to passion.

Isla Mujeres

There's an arch in your heart,
a deserted landscape langours
steeped in the weight of the sea.
Waiting. Enough of the coral
sand, white elephant sheen,
my pelvis pressed between the pages
of your knees. In the cavity
wind blows through, that part
of you that never stays,
like the fixed portions of a blown
through past. I can not change
an absence that is
a space, a whistle-whittled
pain, or ever wish it. Just long
Mayan paths to trace, my indigenous
toes starched with salt, my Purépacha
spine erect, ignorant of your long gone
sex. My brown dog stirs, agitates,
displays. I think I'm a part of you
but its only celestial, nothing
reflecting the blue. If you were
a man like a rock you could fill,
stave, remember: how our poverty
sticks, how a spirit saves, how frank
the powers are in the ancient
sprays, the perfumed rock, a ruined
sun and the devil wind – a matrimony.

A un Desconocido

I was looking for your hair,
black as old lava on an island
of white coral. I dreamed it
deserted you and came for me,
wrapped me in its funeral ribbons
and tied me a bow of salt.

Here's where I put my demise:
desiring fire in a web of tide,
marrying the smell of wet ashes
to the sweet desert of your slate.
My intelligent mammal, male
of my species, twin sun to a world
not of my making, you reduce me
to the syrup of the moon, you boil
my bones in the absence of hands.

Where is your skin, parting me?
Where is the cowlick under your kiss
teasing into purple valleys? Where
are your wings, the imaginary tail
and its exercise? Where would I breed
you? In the neck of my secret heart
where you'll go to the warmth of me
biting into that bread where crumbs crack
and scatter and feed us our souls;

if only you were a stone I could
throw, if only I could have you.

Irresistible

Skip the bread.
Grow a garden.
And I will chalk
in a sky light as
ocean, stunning
as full sun after
mass, the church
steeple, yellow
in the fading
cellophane glow.
Can you laugh
in the face of
our viscous
tentacles? You,
shy man, wary
and wiry as lobster
after storm. Can
you cry out with
wishing for the
tongue, for the
hunger? Come,
and let us eat
up the hours
between us.

Canto 38

I dream of a house
where the water seeps
through the floorboards,
that speaks to me in a creaking
vocabulary of lust, that shakes
me out in a sun-drenched plaza
where I drift like the invisible dead
or the noisy cats stiffened with crusts.

I rise and eat lace
through the fuchsias of my dreams.
I invent myself past butterflies
of extinct corals. I imagine
a mouth that might gnaw
through the hunger of orchids
to a vast exchange
of currency and coin,
rigid and tinned with
the taste of blood sacrifice.
My sex, like a fine down
pillow, stays stuffed in its sack
through episodes of missed arousals.

What if I never unfurl?
What if my skin won't scurry
with the furry fire ants of paradise?
(They are so tiny! Willing earthquakes
of dust!) What if the black
frigate bird at my vulva
sways her rare wings

in a sudden rush of desire,
deadly as the far reddening tide?
I age quickly in struts
and thumps like a rusted spring.
I rearrange myself, straddle
the faceless horses of the moment
pushed against the limits
of my thighs. Whose life
would it save, this frayed bag
with its plumage sticking out
from the seams? Were you
a blizzard, I would be
useless as toast, soaked
to the bone-sucked stitches.

Overhead, chubascos of military
tanks and their armor rev up the hemisphere.
Palms bend, supplicant but wary;
and the mangoes in their carts splatter
the stony rain with their fragrance
of decay, an unused perfume, a wasted
spray, a forgotten melody drifting
on the page like a love
letter – undeliverable, but licked.

Suite: Fall

1.

How could I have let it go?
A sun-tipped feather falls,
aspens age, the treeline recedes
in early snow. The falcons rear
their young alone, the hunter
falters by the stream and new
scat glistens beside the last
wild raspberries. So sweet, a
mouth once touched me here.
Another, never. No passion
left on the bough, a final
quiver as earth-breath shakes
the losers. In a steady first rain
void of flash and rumble, the wet
dirt chooses her seed and lets,
allows, seeps. I refold the yellow
tablet pages, press the seams
the way I've never kneaded you.

2.

Fall. The garden reaches for another
bloom, cosmos leans towards winter,
lettuce aches to seed. Where
once the stabbing mouths of birds
fed hunger, now only the migrating
vultures shadow, return. Too long
I've needed graphite, secrets, memory.

3.

I wake to you, death on the mind.
The ocean between us is really
the wind crashing onto shore, the height
rolling onto the breadth of plain. You,
opening in sleep, gigantic fleshy
flower of man. Like all men,
you sleep best in the petals of woman.

4.

An ancient traveler, the volleys
of pure, unexcitable wind
engorges the canyon. Unseasonable
heat turns the panes of current,
guns the engines of howling trees;
no matter how all in a circle of God
encloses the storm. An old-fashioned
calm domesticates the funnel. I,
in my patterned robe, stall to immobile
the backwards counting of my personal
dead. This one refused to rest. No one
claimed the body, a common-law daughter
denied the relation. What did he have
but a clock and a flare? Some glimpsed,
some missed, some still sing in the night,
a wolf's hour prowling. What doesn't translate
gets lost in the forward shuffle, grunting
like these sycamores threatening to leave.
What is between us still lashes, straining
the claim. One weak note fazes the gaze
like this hammer of gale. Never a hand

or a fist; not a death, the gravest string
on a sonnet to savagery; memory.

5.

I make myself the bridge, paused in the miraculous
lifting swelling to sky, just-fledged. Through you
the natural boundaries gain weight. My circle
of states lean on the darkness beside me.
The simplest acts hesitate, break all the moving,
all the mad imagination of a twister ready to kill.
Man-meat, heaving fist of sleep, star-limbed
dreamer thrumming with the bitch's leg,
                                        I understand you
when you wake to me shedding sheets
like a disposal of age, your anger, deep,
a dangling nest. The sedentary trees,
useless as rage. The leaving, twisted
memory.

Socorro

for Jim (1948 – 4/6/98)

Death is a noun, the rain murmurs,
but to love is forever a verb.

— Jim Sagel

I envied you,
that sapling fence,
how you stripped
and heaved each young
green shoot of its
treasure of golden
telling tongues.
How you rerooted
the sturdy stakes, plunged
each bone leg, ivory
as your hands, into the good
rusting Española earth
you loved – and rerouted
a singular Colorado boyhood
on the wheated plain.

Yes,
there was the dusted
chafing of aging
sandstone, the watered down
mud of your self-made
house, the adobe walls
aged into rock. But it
wasn't the sanctuary
of stone that you listened

to nightly that impressed
me, it was how you made
the displaced sheaves
of tree skin sing, how
you fingered the graphite
sticks between an outstretched
thumb and an index
and blackened in
the eyes and mouths
of a people. I loved
how the wind whistled
through the gaps
in the lines, how many
voices gathered there
in your tender gathering.
All the shunned leaves
whispering like the ghosts
of those gone, all
the passed on poets
who never wrote
a word: articulate
and present in a thirst-
struck land. At your hand –
the Seven Caves of Cíbola,
inconsequential as gold.

Now, the swords of yucca
are conquered with a fine white
dye, and the ancianos o piñones
of "St. Lawrence" are awe struck
and cold, and the bitter
herbs of Passover stun
the tongue with the taste
for sanctuary or socorro.

I look for you in all
the left behind aspens,
or in a slender collection
you signed one winter:
Amiga y compañera
en esta 'movida'
de la vida. All the fine
limned pain belongs
to another, all the stories
you heard and plucked
and pressed into unfading color
among the pages. Only one poem
sings a song of yourself:
a poem for your father's
hands of so large and silent
a love . . . hands so scarred by
water and earth, and your father's
mother who lost all the songs
of her mother, and now a hand
that has held nothing but pencil
. . . so smooth and unmarked a hand
that has never held love but as a book
at a readable

distance.

In the distance, a parched
wilderness for the lonely hunter
leaving behind him a memory
of the fallen families shivering
under coin and the golden blood
of dusk. Under the warming
sky, in the cruelest month,
a living sap still touches
the lips, and feels

an old surge through
the withering veins at the roots.
And the leaves of your books
are left here for the younger
saplings, those born or grafted
onto the largest family on the planet –
for poetry, like an aspen, is the hugest
being on earth. Even though you
left us, alone, with a note and a lack,
mouthing in the radioactive wind
of an untranslatable
word: *Socorro.*

Archeology

I can't keep my hands from stones,
rocks of another age, chipped obsidian
blades, jagged monsters etched in sea
jade, graying zebras of hieroglyphs,
small black eyes of agate, saved
Indian signs chiseled from my kin. I rise
with the weight of loaded-down pockets;
all your buried treasures like a loose
hard-on knocking against my thigh, an old
woman's jewels in her empty house, a womb
alone in the pouch of my flesh.
                                        Here's for you
to find: a comb with a few silver threads,
a map to the caves where spirals
of heaven print scarves on the shale, where
digits of splayed testimony plant their red
mark upon the diamonded granite, where the older
bloodstone, sand-dappled, reveals the ravaged
river shrimp; here in the brine of history
and pulverized bone, I find my sinker,
discover the leaden lure as ancestral
graves give out; and I endure.

In an Eagle's Nestling

We took no photograph
of that fledgling peace;
a graph upon a map, a salmon
sun, raw upon the horizon, blessed
us. That maître d' of the soul's
arrival. Spirit dressed in a flag, a drape,
a shroud agape upon the flyer:
that bird as symbol, a flap of heart.
Would it serve? Here, now, learning
to speak, to soar. We were learning to begin,
too sore. We were learning to begin,
again – that constant rolling
up the matted nights, the constant
rowing toward the shore of what
we think we desire. That bird.
That beast of a State. That veil.
A fingerless ring hawing up
through a recital of wings.
This bird. This heart. Dear heart,
deer hearted in the distance
once. I tell you, autumn sings
in the betrayal
of proximity – one edge
too far; another, the darker
sister, a mother of another –
you deciding. All of that.
A bird I didn't catch, there
on the side of a mountain
lake I didn't drive us to:
your breath, a hair
away from me. All of me

beneath the shadow of a dime,
home to a shadow of crime.
You, loving that accounts
manager of some made
for life movie, that soccer mom
of the what-should-I-do

now

that a spark of freedom
flared there in that nest;
you and me, and some setting
that has us sitting out the part;
a new beginning in the world
and chaste, too chaste,
this sometime used to be –
now alive and breathing
here beside a Rocky shore
of more, more open, more
mouth, more noticing.
As I held you, a bird
was learning to open the wind,
to trust. Again. Us, a new
honeymoon, a new date
on the calendar of lust
and fulfillment, same sullen
thing – no more. Hope on a
wing. Freedom in a word
breathed heavily in;
and it takes. Oxygen relieved
through the trees, those officiates
of this marriage to the will
of a world which allows us
to see. "I love you"
in a world, in a bird.

Author's Note

I am influenced by painters. Irving Norman, in particular, whom I once met when I was about 18 after I had written a poem about one of the major images in his show, face-masks, that was exhibiting in the San José State Student Union gallery. I was giving a poetry reading and read the poem. He was there, and when I looked up and said his name, I gave him a copy of the poem. He invited me to a party closing the show. There, a young woman questioned him before a tryptic (think Bosch): three individual paintings which create another composition, another solid image, when hung together – of a futuristic warscape, mostly blood and ash colored, dominated by armies of armored behemuths that must have inspired *Star Wars*. She asked him: "Do you really see the world this way? Just brutality & greed? Do you really believe that people can be so awful?" And he just cried. Silent tears streaming down his face for an uncomfortable 20 minutes. What a number on an arm can tell about a paint smear on cloth. An artist only paints what he sees. An artist only paints what she was meant to see. Intent. The after-image of grey felt by Beuys blooms into a colored mural in someone else's life a continent away, a heart away. That close.

I am not driven, so much, by intentions, as I am stunned into being by intent.

One starlit October night I was sitting with my dear friend, Dylan Morgan. Dylan of the wide Texas mind. Dylan who first introduced me to Eduardo Galeano's *Memoria del fuego*. Dylan who read books and painted everyday. A friend of his had copied all of his paintings for the year, some 400 of them, and they were placing them in small binders. I looked through all of them; some I knew from the painting of them, some from their description or the set they belonged to: Kathe Kollwitz, Tamayo, contemporary photo-docs, . . . I stopped at a small painting of a man playing the violin seated among the espinas of cacti in a field of Van Gogh yellow. Something about his face, some challenge: to do! I set it in front of me. I wanted to buy that painting. Next was a blurry vision of boys & drunk men in a cantina. Next, a faceless war scene – a man holding the lifeless body of a child. The last was one of the last in the pile: "DRIVE!" I thought – a woman wearing my grandmother's scarf on her head holding her hands in front of her on the steering wheel of the go-nowhere car. I stared into that pic, those starfish hands, deciding. Somewhere inside, the printer in me, the craftperson, my grandmother, said: "This would make a great cover!" (Something about the immediacy of the "arrow" on the right that drives one to act, to open.) And I laid it out on the floor in front of me with the others – in the form of a Tarot cross. I was moving to Boulder. It was always my intention to purchase some of Dylan's paintings. Soon I would have a salary. Dylan interrupted my ruminating by handing me a book by Argentinian poet-in-exile, Juan Gelman. I opened it at random to a poem that would change my life forever, that's how much it spoke to me: "You Are." I sat there, stunned, gonging, my thoughts in a stammer. I picked up the four and gazed at them, in the order they appear in this book. Not deciding. At the last, I said again, thinking of my favorite lived line of poetry by Robert Creeley: "DRIVE!"

And knew I had a book. I had four. And, a face.

The books are intended to be read in any order the reader desires. They are bound together in this edition for affordability and for carrying them with you, perhaps, like me, under some tree. Bound so that you don't have to worry about getting them dirty, books intended to be consumed with wine & cheese, pita & hummus, Soyrizo & tortillas organicas. A book that could serve as a table, a plate, a platform.

They are all, like us, distinctly different from each other but linked to some common phenomenology, some base language of Spirit where we thrive, an inheritance of disparate images, the over-abundance of flowering & decay under history & chance; this United State.

For Dad, Visionary Artist, Luis Cervantes (11/1/23-4/27/05).

– Lorna Dee Cervantes

About the Author

A fifth generation Californian of Mexican and Native American (Chumash) heritage, Lorna Dee Cervantes was a pivotal figure throughout the Chicano literary movement She began publishing the literary journal *Mango* in 1976. Her small press, also named Mango, was widely admired for its creative designs and for the important voices it brought into print, including Sandra Cisneros, Gary Soto, Luis Omar Salinas, and Alberto Ríos.

Her poetry has appeared in literally hundreds of literary magazines and she has been featured on the cover of *Bloomsbury Review* and other literary journals. Her work has also been included in many anthologies, including *Daughters of the Fifth Sun* (1995), *¡Floricanto Sí! A Collection of Latina Poetry* (Penguin, 1998), *Unsettling America: An Anthology of Contemporary Multicultural Poetry* (1994), *No More Masks! An Anthology of Twentieth-Century Women Poets* (1993), and *After Aztlan: Latino Poets of the Nineties* (1992). Cervantes' poems have appeared in over 150 textbooks, including mainstays such as *The Norton Anthology of American Literature* and *The Heath Anthology of American Literature.*

Cervantes' first book, *Emplumada* (University of Pittsburgh, 1981), a recipient of the American Book Award, was praised as "a seamless collection of poems that move back and forth between the gulf of desire and possibility." Her second collection, *From the Cables of Genocide: Poems on Love and Hunger* (Arte Público, 1991) was awarded the Patterson Poetry Prize, the poetry prize of the Institute of Latin American Writers, and the Latino Literature Award. In 1995 she received a Lila Wallace-Reader's Digest Writers' Award.

Cervantes holds an A.B.D. in the History of

Consciousness; she is an associate professor of English at the University of Colorado in Boulder where, until recently, she directed the creative writing program. She has received two National Endowment for the Arts poetry fellowships and a Lila Wallace Readers Digest Fellowship.

Lorna Dee invites anyone who is interested to visit her blog at http://lornadice.blogspot.com

About the Artists

Irving **Norman** was born Irving Noachowitz in 1906. He emigrated from Poland, now Lithuania, to the United States in 1923. Through the Depression years Irving worked as a barber in New York and devoted much of his spare time to left-wing political causes. His deeply felt sociopolitical awareness led him in 1938 to the join the Abraham Lincoln Brigade and fight in the Spanish Civil War. This experience was the catalyst that sparked a fifty-year creative legacy that produced a vast number of drawings, watercolors and oil paintings of immense size and complex detail. Irving lived and painted in the San Francisco Bay Area and passed away in the summer of 1989. For more information: www.irving-norman.com

Dylan **Morgan** is an admitted anti-technologist. Born in Dallas, Texas, in 1955, he was educated at San Jose State University in Philosophy and Music. As a jazz drummer, he studied in New York with Milford Graves and recorded in San Francisco with saxophonist Sonny Simmons. He did two US tours as cellist/music director with Chicago-based performance poet Daniel X. O'Neil. Morgan has been painting since 1984, with exhibitions in Chicago, Los Angeles and elsewhere. His portrait of poet Greg Keith (1945-1998) appeared in his book *Life Near 310 Kelvin* (SLG Books, 1998). Morgan collects (and reads) rare books.

Colophon

This first edition of *Drive: The First Quartet*, by Lorna Dee Cervantes, has been printed on 70 pound paper containing fifty percent recycled fiber. The text has been set in using Adobe Caslon type. Section and poem titles have been set in Cochin. This book was designed by Lorna Dee Cervantes and Bryce Milligan.

The blind impression on the front of *Drive* is taken from a Chumash pictograph in a cave in San Marcos Pass, California.

The first 100 signature sets to be pulled from the press have been numbered and signed, specially bound, and boxed in hand-made wooden boxes.

Drive: The First Quartet made its early debut in October 2005 with a performance at the National Museum of Women in the Arts in Washington, D.C.

What we call the beginning is often the end
And to make an end is to make a beginning.

– T. S. Eliot

c/s